TUBA SKINNY AI

By

Pops Coffee

Copyright © 2017

Table of Contents

INTRODUCTION 5
TUBA SKINNY – WORLD LEADERS 6
HOW DO THEY DO IT?..16
WHAT HAPPENED AFTER AFTER KATRINA................24
TUBA SKINNY AT HOME IN NOLA 29
SHAYE COHN..35
SHAYE'S MOZARTIAN QUALITIES 41
SHAYE THE COMPOSER..43
SHAYE AS PERFORMANCE DIRECTOR 45
SETTING THE TEMPO 46
TODD AND BARNABUS 48
BARNABUS AND GLISSANDI...50
BARNABUS SINGS 52
ROBIN RAPUZZI 53
CHARLIE HALLORAN..56
TUBA SKINNY'S CD - 'OWL CALL BLUES' 58
TUBA SKINNY'S CD - 'BLUE CHIME STOMP' 61
TUBA SKINNY'S CD - 'TUPELO PINE' 66
MAKING MUCH OUT OF SIMPLE MATERIAL...............70
A VISIT TO BACCHANAL 72
'ALLIGATOR CRAWL' 74
'ALL I WANT IS A SPOONFUL' 79
'ALMOST AFRAID TO LOVE'...81
'BEER GARDEN BLUES' 83
'BELLAMINA' 85

'BLUE CHIME STOMP' 88
ERIKA'S 'BROKEN-HEARTED BLUES' 90
'CHOCOLATE AVENUE' 92
'CRAZY BLUES' 93
'CRAZY 'BOUT YOU' 97
'DALLAS RAG' 98
'DANGEROUS BLUES' 99
'DEAR ALMANZOER' 103
'DEEP HENDERSON' 104
'DELTA BOUND' 105
'DODO BLUES' 106
'DO YOUR DUTY' 107
'DUSTY RAG' 108
'FINGERING WITH YOUR FINGERS' 110
TUBA SKINNY AND MEMPHIS MINNIE 112
FROM 'CALL OF THE FREAKS' TO 'GARBAGE MAN'115
'HE LIKES IT SLOW' 117
'HILARITY RAG' 119
'I'M BLUE AND LONESOME' 121
'JACKSON STOMP' AND 'CROW JANE' 123
'LATE HOUR BLUES', 'MEMPHIS SHAKE' AND 'MICHIGANDER BLUES' 126
'NEED A LITTLE SUGAR IN MY BOWL' 129
'OWL CALL BLUES' 132
'ORIENTAL STRUT' 134
'POSTAGE STOMP' 137
'PYRAMID STRUT' 139

'SALAMANCA BLUES'..143
'SKID DAT DE DAT' 145
'SOMEBODY'S BEEN LOVING MY BABY' 147
'TANGLED BLUES' AND 'THOUGHTS'............................148
'TRICKS AIN'T WALKING NO MORE' 151
THE REPERTOIRE 152
About The Author..167

INTRODUCTION

I discovered Tuba Skinny in 2010 when a friend recommended a couple of their videos on YouTube. Within a few weeks, after watching many more videos, I was convinced that Tuba Skinny was the best band playing traditional jazz anywhere in the world.

I followed their progress closely and their music gave me enormous pleasure.

When I visited New Orleans in April 2015, I finally got to hear the band in person. On that occasion and on a couple of subsequent visits, I also had the pleasure of making some videos of their performances and also meeting members of the band.

This book is an appreciation of their wonderful music. And it is especially an appreciation of Shaye Cohn, who is the band's unofficial Musical Director.

TUBA SKINNY – WORLD LEADERS

Let me tell you straight away that Tuba Skinny is currently considered by many people to be the best traditional jazz band playing anywhere in the world today. Judge for yourself by going to YouTube and watching the short video labelled 'Tuba Skinny @ Duke Heitger 4th Annual Steamboat Stomp, 23-25 September, 2016' (https://www.youtube.com/watch?v=NfH2g_yRrpQ). It was made in late 2016 and is to be commended for its fine sound and visual qualities. We have to thank the video-maker codenamed CANDCJ for this treat. But if you are able to settle to an entire well-filmed concert by the band (it runs for an hour and a half), there is an excellent video on Vimeo entitled 'Tuba Skinny Wealthy Theatre March 3 2016'. It is at: https://vimeo.com/234914190.

Although they have appeared elsewhere in the USA, notably around New York, and also have toured in several countries, including Mexico, Sweden, Australia, Switzerland, France, Italy and Spain, they spend half their year busking in the streets and playing in the clubs of New Orleans, their natural setting. By 2017 they had been playing together for seven years and had recorded 8 CDs.

The musicians appear content to live mainly on the income from busking. They seem to live cheaply, using bicycles for most transport needs. Yes, even their wonderful singer Erika (who has since moved away from New Orleans) used to get around with her bass drum on her bicycle. Trombonist Barnabus can often be seen taking his trombone and Tupelo, the band's internationally-renowned dog (the group's Chief Executive!), on his bicycle trailer.

Tuba Skinny plays jazz in the style established in New Orleans and Chicago between 1900 and 1930. The musicians have built up a wide repertoire, mixing classics (especially blues) with more modern tunes, including original compositions. They have rescued from near-obscurity such 90-year-old gems as *Muddy Water, New Orleans Stomp, Russian Rag, New Orleans Bump, Deep Henderson, Chocolate Avenue, Frog Hop, Variety Stomp, Dear Almanzoer, Harlem's Araby* and *Minor Drag*; and the Jabbo Smith forgotten classics from the 1920s - *Michigander Blues* and *Sleepy Time Blues* and *A Jazz Battle.* They have shown, with their fresh and original interpretations, how exciting these tunes can be.

How do they decide on their repertoire? In an interview, percussionist Robin Rapuzzi explained: 'It's a group decision. It always is. Tuba Skinny is a miniature political system of majority rule. We discuss ideas with each other either on the street or over dinner. We have listening-parties throughout the year to discuss what we're interested in and where we want to go with our music. It's very organic. We're very fortunate to all be so interested in the same kind of music and to have met each other when and where we did and with a travelling itch and desire to busk'.

The songs are played against a rock-steady 'walking' rhythm, with tuba, washboard, guitar and/or banjo laying down the foundation while the cornet, trombone and clarinet play the melody and frolic around it. For its first three years, the band had no reed player (except when a welcome guest sat in), so there was a distinctive brassy sound.

In the streets, there is no use of the electronic amplification that spoils so much music these days.

Tunes do not outstay their welcome: most are completed in about four minutes. This is because the musicians of Tuba Skinny avoid the dreary succession of uninspired solo choruses that we associate with many other traditional jazz bands. Usually, in a 32-bar chorus, two or more instruments take the lead for a few bars each.

The Band's remarkable singer - Erika Lewis - grew up in New York State's Hudson Valley. She has been compared with Bessie Smith (who must have been her inspiration) and in my opinion she equals the great Bessie in vocal ability. In street performances she needs no microphone. Since 2012, Erika has also taken to playing the bass drum, on which she sits as she sings and plays - further solidifying the band's rhythm section. Erika has said (*Offbeat Magazine*, September 2014), 'It just dawned on me one day that a bass drum was something that I could add and it would fit in. For the first year, I strapped it to my front, but I felt like a pregnant spider flailing around, standing up while everyone else was sitting down. So I said, *I'm just going to sit down on it*.'

There is a vocal in about 75% of the tunes played by the band, and these are mostly performed by Erika, though other members also contribute.

At the end of 2015, to the disappointment of her many fans, Erika moved away from New Orleans and therefore ceased appearing with the band in the New Orleans streets. But she has continued to appear with the band at festivals and on tours.

Tuba Skinny is a model collective enterprise, without a star or prima donna. But I must admit a special admiration of Shaye Cohn, the young lady who plays the cornet and generally directs the musical traffic.

As one who attempts to play the jazz cornet myself, I appreciate her technical virtuosity and amazing inventiveness. Using mutes with great skill, she produces a unique tone that perfectly encapsulates the blues feeling that is at the heart of so much of our music. She knows just when to bend notes and she has a great instinct for bluesy notes in the right places. Her phrasing is impeccable. Shaye is not a showy player who produces lots of high and raucous notes, like so many traditional jazz band trumpeters. Her playing is busy, but in an unobtrusive way. Just listen to her extraordinarily inventive and subtle improvisations and don't miss the way she provides brilliant delicate arabesques behind the solos of others (such as the trombone - which often takes the melody), and particularly behind the singer.

I have been told that, when she was just nine years old, Shaye was a member of The New England Conservatory Children's Chorus and sang solo on stage. This amazing lady from Boston is classically trained (she graduated in Music at New York University) and, as YouTube demonstrates, also plays other instruments (especially the accordion, violin and piano - and even the spoons!) brilliantly. Shaye is also currently one of the best traditional jazz piano-players on the New Orleans scene, even though she generally prefers to play the cornet. She even produces the delightful artwork for the band's CD covers. What a talented lady!

The guitarist when the band was formed was Kiowa Wells and he and the slim Todd Burdick (tuba - Mr. Tuba Skinny in person - originally from Chicago) were the founders of the band, building it up by inviting other fine musicians they met busking on the streets of New Orleans.

There used to be a magnificent, bulky, brilliant tuba player known as *Tuba Fats* who could be heard busking and playing in the clubs of New Orleans. His real name was Anthony Lacen. He died in 2004 at the age of only 53. I heard him once – in a busking group on Jackson Square.

Unlike him, tuba-player Todd Burdick is tall and slender. So it was a great idea to nickname him 'Tuba Skinny'. A band called *Tuba Skinny and His Tiny Men* emerged. But it took no time at all before the entire band became known as Tuba Skinny.

The original Tuba Skinny musicians were (circa 2007) part of the band *Loose Marbles*, a musical collective that still exists but that spawned several of the great bands based in New Orleans today. Todd and Kiowa are very skilful, sensitive and accurate players. You quickly notice from their early recordings how thoroughly they learned their music, how meticulously they prepared and played. Todd originally played guitar and banjo (as he still does when required) and he is very good on those instruments. It must be a big help to be strong in your knowledge of chord sequences when laying a secure foundation on the tuba. Listen carefully to the tuba in Tuba Skinny performances and notice how solid and accurate is the foundation Todd lays and how important this is to the special sound of the band.

Kiowa occasionally sang; and he also contributed some fine guitar solo choruses.

But Ryan Baer on banjo and guitar replaced Kiowa after a year or so. Ryan is extremely good, whether providing rhythmic support or delicate melodic solo choruses. He too is a fine singer.

And in later months, other guitar and banjo players have been frequently used. Guitarist Max Bien-Kahn from Oregon, who has also frequently worked as the band's recording engineer, has provided a rock-solid rhythmic backing in hundreds of performances, and toured with the band. Since 2014 such fine and well-known New Orleans street performers as Gregory Sherman and Jason Lawrence (and occasionally Stalebread Scottie) played on banjo and guitar. Another fine player who appeared occasionally on tenor banjo was the Texan Westen Borghesi. To appreciate Westen's very skilful and sympathetic playing, listen carefully to his contribution throughout the band's CD called *Pyramid Strut*.

No matter who plays, they all conform to the Tuba Skinny house style - laying down a very solid four-to-the-bar foundation. The combination of Todd Burdick on tuba and a guitar player (such as Max Bien-Kahn) provides a powerful engine that drives the band along; and all the banjo players over the years have been brilliant at maintaining that rock-steady rhythm.

The ever-present trombonist (except when he headed off on a sailing cruise in early 2016!) is the versatile Barnabus Jones, who possesses a big sound and has mastered the tricks of Kid Ory, John Thomas, Honoré Dutrey and Fred Robinson - the trombonists who played with Louis Armstrong in the 1920s. He has developed a great tone that perfectly matches that of Shaye. It is a tone that gives a sense of power under control, with the slight raspiness so valuable in playing traditional jazz. Barnabus produces musical phrases that perfectly complement Shaye's melodic inventions. The trombone and cornet blend magically. What is more, Barnabus is also a very fine player of the banjo and the violin, which were his original instruments; and on occasion he shows himself to be no mean singer!

All the Tuba Skinny instruments are easily portable. This is particularly helpful if you are a street band. They often have no drum kit, for example. But they have a washboard player – Robin Rapuzzi from Seattle (though I'm proud to report his mother was born in England). Normally, I am not keen on the washboard as a musical instrument: I have known a badly-played washboard to wreck a jazzband, especially when the player fails to keep a steady tempo. But Mr. Rapuzzi is a great driving force for the rhythm of this band, and fully underpins the music's structures. He has fixed a few additional small percussive items to his washboard, so he can produce tricky crowd-pleasing solo choruses, with sound varied very imaginatively.

Although it's easier to play a washboard on the street than to lug around a full drum kit, Robin was originally a drummer, and enjoys the full range of tones and colours that he can get from the drum kit, including the snare and Chinese tom-drum and Chinese-crash cymbal. He used a full drum kit when making the band's 7th CD; and at the end of 2015 he managed to start taking a full kit along to street busking – pedalling a bicycle with a trailer - which he described as 'some kind of work out'!

On a few occasions (including a tour to Mexico), the wonderful washboard player Defne Incirlioglu deputised for Robin.

There are other part-time members of this band – too numerous for me to track or mention. In their videos you may spot an occasional double bass, or violin, or a second trumpet. This is bound to happen with a street busking band. But I must tell you that a young lady called Alynda Lee Segarra (who now mostly tours with her own band) used to play banjo and sing very well.

But most of the fine young musicians of New Orleans have played in the band at some time or other. Another has been Albanie Falletta on guitar; and the great and ubiquitous Charlie Halloran (trombone) sometimes deputises for Barnabus.

Ewan Bleach from the U.K. on clarinet and saxophone fitted in brilliantly for a year or so (Ewan is incidentally also a superb jazz pianist); and John Doyle on sax and clarinet is another fine player (reminiscent of Jimmy Noone) who settled well into the band during 2013 when they were playing some of their greatest music. These two are outstandingly good musicians. Just listen closely to their work in any of the videos and you will class them among the very best traditional jazz reed-men you have ever encountered.

Jonathan Doyle studied briefly at Depaul's School of Music in Chicago and has worked with several bands, including his own quintet. He now divides his time between Chicago, Austin and spells with Tuba Skinny - in New Orleans and touring abroad. He is also a composer of music for his bands.

(By the way, Jonathan Doyle and Westen Borghesi both play in the wonderful *Thrift Set Orchestra* in Austin, Texas. There are some videos of this group - well worth watching - on YouTube.)

From 2014 onwards, the reed player has most frequently been Craig Flory, from Seattle; and from the end of 2015, Tomas Majcherski, the very fine player from *The Smoking Time Jazz Club* band, was also regularly helping out on reeds.

Tuba Skinny dress and present themselves in a laid-back, smart-casual manner. The gents wear baseball caps and – on hot days – play in singlets and shorts, without shirts. The ladies have a penchant for short socks and flat shoes or trainers. So they have perfect looks for a New Orleans street band; and they tend to dress similarly for indoor gigs – bringing a breath of fresh air into what might otherwise be stuffy or formal venues. They are surprisingly modest, unassuming young people, having fun playing the music they love and scarcely aware of their own enormous talent.

But please let me beg you to try this band for yourself! There are over 500 examples of their work on YouTube.

You might care to go way back in time and start by typing into YouTube 'Tuba Skinny - Hear me talkin - Live at the Hive 6-24-2011' (https://www.youtube.com/watch?v=zMsgz4wHWF4)

Here you can meet the band in a relaxed, undemanding, gentle-tempo 12-bar blues in the Key of C. The tune (made famous by Ma Rainey) is *Hear Me Talkin' To Ya*. Unfortunately the camera does not catch much of Robin (washboard) but you have good examples of everything else, including brief solos from tuba and guitar.

Try the band here in its original formation in a quicker number. Type 'Tuba Skinny at Bearsville Theater Six Feet Down' into YouTube (https://www.youtube.com/watch?v=vQM5JGKGlAI). This song – *Six Feet Down* - was written by Erika Lewis, who is seen singing it. The video illustrates much of what I have been saying (including – note – the skilful washboard playing) and you can identify all six of the original core members of *Tuba Skinny*.

And *Garbage Man* is a terrific, infectious, fun number. You can watch it (with Ewan and John on reeds) by typing 'Tuba Skinny - Garbage Man - Spotted Cat 4-10-12' (https://www.youtube.com/watch?v=kQDP2tdNFKY).

To hear an example of Shaye Cohn's brilliance, even when she had been learning to play the cornet for only a year or so, listen to her solo that comes one minute and fifteen seconds into this next video. Quite apart from its technical virtuosity and fireworks, note its almost surreal inventiveness, especially in the first few bars. Type 'Tuba Skinny at Wild Hive Farm on 9/5/2010 Some of these Days' (https://www.youtube.com/watch?v=6ekgkT6VEHw).

To me it is so thrilling that YOUNG people are keeping alive the traditional jazz of New Orleans. I was there in 1998, and many of the great musicians of those pre-Katrina days have since passed on. But – thanks to groups like Tuba Skinny – their music has not disappeared with them.

Now listen to their wonderful and energetic performance of *Minor Drag* three years later: type 'Tuba Skinny - Minor drag - Rapperswil 30 juni 2013' (https://www.youtube.com/watch?v=J_jB_WbPg9I).

HOW DO THEY DO IT?

How has it come about that Tuba Skinny – a group of surprisingly young musicians – whose founder members met in 2008 while busking on the streets of New Orleans, has become the greatest traditional jazz band in the world today?

Here are some of the answers.

All the musicians in the group have thoroughly mastered their instruments; and most of them can play more than one (e.g. cornet + piano + violin; tuba + banjo; trombone + banjo; banjo + harmonica + mandolin + guitar). This provides variety of sound and also the ability to substitute if a regular player is unavailable.

They prefer collective improvisation to prima donna solos. Their teamwork is exemplary.

Although they could play the familiar well-worn tunes of every trad band's repertoire, their programmes mostly comprise exciting unfamiliar gems they have unearthed from the 1920s and 1930s (e.g. *New Orleans Bump*, *You Can Have My Husband*, *Chocolate Avenue*, *Jackson Stomp*, *Deep Henderson*, *Banjoreno*, *Treasures Untold*, *Russian Rag*, *Oriental Strut*, *Minor Drag*, *Michigander Blues*, *Harlem's Araby*, *Me and My Chauffeur*, *A Jazz Battle*, *Droppin' Shucks*, *Fourth Street Mess Around*, *Carpet Alley Breakdown*). The almost-forgotten artists whose music they have revived include Lucille Bogan, Victoria Spivey, Memphis Minnie, Jabbo Smith, Georgia White, Skip James, Merline Johnson, Ma Rainey, Hattie Hart, The Memphis Jug Band, Blind Blake, Clara Smith, The Dixieland Jug Blowers, The Grinnell Giggers and The Mississippi Mud Steppers; and of course they also play tunes associated with the better-known, such as Bessie Smith, Fats Waller, Louis Armstrong and Jelly Roll

Morton. They will surprise you by going to some unconventional sources for tunes they turn into exciting traditional jazz - sources such as Ray Charles and the 21st-century Australian original C. W. Stoneking.

They have an outstandingly good singer (Erika Lewis). She has a soulful plaintive voice and great intonation. Her phrasing is perfect and she uses rubato very skilfully. Rather than stick to the familiar jazz standards, she has developed a rich repertoire of tunes rescued from obscurity (e.g. *Tricks Ain't Walking*, *Crow Jane*, *How Do They Do It That Way?*, *Mississippi River Blues*, *I'll See You in the Spring*, *Need a Little Sugar in my Bowl*, *You Let Me Down*, *Got a Man in the 'Bama Mines*, *What's the Matter with the Mill?*). Erika also doubles on bass drum.

Other members of Tuba Skinny are also very competent vocalists.

They work very hard behind the scenes – researching and learning the old material and devising ways of playing it with fresh vigour. And they are perfectionists. Look, for example, at their performances of *Deep Henderson*, a tricky multi-part rhythmic piece. While showing respect for the 1926 recording of this tune by King Oliver's Band, Tuba Skinny do not slavishly imitate: they show what they can do with their own resources. They have arranged the piece meticulously. And all members of the band have the arrangement firmly inside their heads. They know exactly who does what, and when. And they also know where they have a chance to cut loose for a few bars. Now watch other bands playing this tune. Almost invariably they are dependent on printed arrangements on music stands in front of them, and their performances sound far less exciting and more stilted.

(By the way, for those of you who have never studied how music is written down, let me explain that it is divided into units called 'bars' here in England, though I think the Americans prefer the term 'measures'. The majority of jazz tunes are made up of 16 or 32 bars, with each bar consisting of four beats. In this book, I shall have to refer frequently to 'bars', so I hope I have made clear what I mean, and that American readers will understand that 'bars' are the same as 'measures'.)

In many traditional jazz bands, the drumming has a smudging effect, filling every space and sometimes forcing other players to blow too loud. But Robin Rapuzzi, the percussionist, plays in a very discreet and sensitive manner, whether using his full kit or the simple washboard. As a result, there is a clean sound to the rhythm. The musicians of Tuba Skinny allow you to hear clearly the part played by every single instrument: there is no need for anyone to over-blow; and there is none of the muddying effect you sometimes notice with other bands. When he uses the washboard, Robin is superb is his energy and inventiveness and time-keeping (and I speak as one who used not to care much for washboards as musical instruments).

Tuba Skinny avoid the dreary succession of 32-bar 'solo' choruses from four or more instruments that we so often hear in traditional jazz performances. Usually, two or three players lead for a few bars each in covering a 32-bar theme. In the rare instances of complete solo choruses, Tuba Skinny musicians add colouring behind the soloist, either with musical phrases or by using stop chords or long notes.

Tuba Skinny always start a tune well. They have devised an appropriate introduction for every one of their tunes.

The tuba player Todd Burdick provides a very solid bass line for all tunes. It pays to focus on his contribution and admire its accuracy and solidity.

Barnabus Jones has absorbed the skills and techniques of the great traditional jazz trombonists in the famous recordings of the 1920s. He and Shaye the cornet-player work particularly well together – listening carefully to each other and responding to each other's musical phrases. Reed players (introduced from about 2011 and one of them English, I'm pleased to say) have proved just as skilful.

The band takes great care with the setting of tempos at the start of each tune. Once established, the tempo is maintained with metronomic accuracy. There is none of the speeding up or (worse) the wearying drag-back of tempo that you notice in other bands on YouTube. The combination of Todd Burdick on tuba and a guitar player (such as Max Bien Kahn) provides a powerful engine that drives the band along; and all the banjo players over the years have been brilliant at providing the rock-steady rhythms. The banjoists are good at playing tremolos to add emphasis on stressed notes (as in *Jazz Battle*) or to add pretty decorations (in such tunes as *Memphis Shake* and *Michigander Blues*).

The Band is not afraid of key changes within tunes, sometimes because the tune is written that way, sometimes to play the tune in a key that suits the whole band and then in a key with which the singer is more comfortable (e.g. *How Do They Do It That Way?* and *Delta Bound* and *Dangerous Blues*) and sometimes just for the mischief of it. Have a listen on YouTube to *Cannonball*. Notice what tricks they can play even with a 12-bar blues. Admire the Introduction, the Bridges and the Coda, and especially the three key changes! Type in 'Tuba Skinny - Cannonball - Royal St 4/11/14' (https://www.youtube.com/watch?v=bkfE_LmHZgU).

Tuba Skinny devises interesting endings for its tunes. Listen to their very neat codas.

The cornet player and unofficial director of music, the amazing Shaye Cohn is never flashy in her playing. Shaye is also terrific on piano, violin and accordion - and she even sometimes plays the double bass in the country music group *The Lonesome Doves*. This is a group in which Erika Lewis plays guitar, sings and composes most of the songs. May I recommend that you watch a lovely video in which Shaye sings and plays violin with *The Lonesome Doves*? The song is called 'Black Water' and was composed by Erika. You can find it on YouTube by typing 'The Lonesome Doves – Black Water'. It's in A minor and has the feel of an Irish folk ballad.

Shaye has a Mozartian instinct for what works best: she contributes to ensembles in the same way that the viola contributes to the conversation in Mozart's string quartets. She can bend notes and knows instinctively when to use this trick to the best effect. Full of bluesy notes and demonstrating a very effective use of mutes (notably the plunger and the stone-lined cup), the fluent phrases and harmonies she produces are hugely more interesting and exciting than the raucous high-note solos that many traditional jazz trumpeters think the music requires.

The Band does not stick doggedly to instrumentation that involves a trumpet (or cornet) – clarinet - trombone front line for every tune. Sometimes, their music has elements of bluegrass or klezmer or rhythm and blues; and this can involve a whole tune (e.g. *Russian Rag, Jackson Stomp, Papa's Got Your Bath Water On*) being played without cornet or trombone.

They don't mind including an occasional waltz in their programme – especially when the tune has a special beauty (e.g. *Treasures Untold*, *Sunset Waltz*). These are played lovingly, allowing the melodies to speak for themselves.

The violin is sometimes used – both for melodic and rhythmic effects.

Members of the Band have composed tunes for their group to play (e.g. *Salamanca Blues*, *Owl Call Blues* - a hauntingly beautiful song, *Broken-Hearted Blues*, *Thoughts*, the authentically-1920s-sounding *Nigel's Dream*, *Pyramid Strut* - a potential classic of Mortonesque structure and complexity, *Six Feet Down*, the lovely *Blue Chime Stomp*, the craftily-composed *Tangled Blues* - with a highly unusual 18-bar theme – and the elegiac *Deep Bayou Moan*, which some fans consider the most beautiful melody Shaye has written). These pieces are fully up to the quality of the material from the 1920s that they love so much.

The Band is very skilful with 'breaks' – the element Jelly Roll Morton considered so important in jazz. If you don't know what I mean, I am referring to those phrases (typically two bars) where the whole band stops suddenly, except for one instrument – the clarinet, for example – leaving that player to invent a decorative musical phrase to fill the gap before the band picks up again. Tuba Skinny are particularly good at breaks: there never seems to be any doubt about which player will play the break, and all the other players cut off together. (So many other bands fail in this matter. It is particularly irritating when – for example – a drummer plays right through a clarinettist's break.)

Just like a classical orchestra, they take trouble tuning up. To watch them doing so, type 'Tuba Skinny -Short Dressed Girl -

Royal St 4/11/14' into YouTube (https://www.youtube.com/watch?v=-5gLOQnWK6Q).

Finally, as a demonstration of the above points, listen to the way the band interprets and performs *Delta Bound* on its CD. This is a straightforward 32-bar tune, with a structure of four sets of eight bars. Let's call these four sets A1, A2, B [the middle eight], A3. So how do they make *Delta Bound* specially interesting and different? Here's what they do:

Introduction: In the key of D minor, the full band plays A2; then the trombone plays the melody for B; and then the full band plays A3 (total 24-bar introduction – unusual!).

Song: A sudden switch to the key of G minor! Erika Lewis sings the 32-bar song once right through. In A1 and A2, she is solidly supported by the tuba, banjo and washboard. In B and A3, there is quiet decorative support first from the brass and then from the clarinet.

Next time through: The clarinet improvises on A1 – 8 bars only - while the brass trio play long supporting notes, including crescendos! Then the clarinet improvises on A2. The cornet takes over, improvising the eight bars of B, with lovely tuba support; and then the trombone leads the final 8 bars of the song – A3.

Approaching the End: the return of the singer; but Erika picks up the tune not at the beginning but rather at the middle eight – B, while the clarinet provides decorative background. Then the full band joins in for A3 with long-note harmonies.

Coda: Suddenly we switch back to the opening key - D minor - just for the final eight bars! How cheeky is that? The full band plays A3 again as the coda, with a rallentando to round off.

What about that for an interpretation? How many other traditional jazz bands have such terrific head arrangements?

If you would like to hear this performance of *Delta Bound*, type this into your browser:
http://tubaskinny.bandcamp.com/track/delta-bound

'I think what's unique about our group is that everyone is really dedicated to the music,' said Erika Lewis in an interview. 'That's the bottom line. How we measure success is all about how well we played.'

WHAT HAPPENED AFTER AFTER KATRINA

I live about 4600 miles from New Orleans and have managed to visit the great City only nine times in my life. My visits started in the 1990s, when Preservation Hall was the obvious place to go for top-quality traditional jazz. There was also some good jazz to be heard in several bars and restaurants; and there were quite a few decent busking groups on the streets. The musicians were mainly black and many of them were elderly (and alas have since died: think of Narvin Kimball, Percy and Willie Humphrey, Milton Batiste, Lionel Ferbos, Pud Brown, Danny Barker, Harold Dejan and James Prevost - all of whom I had the pleasure of hearing). But in the 1990s nobody would have thought of Frenchmen Street (at the eastern edge of the French Quarter) as the best place to look for outstanding traditional jazz.

During a visit in 2015, I found the situation had changed dramatically. For example, Frenchmen Street had now become the place to base yourself in the evenings if you wanted the choice of a wide range of top-quality bands playing in various bars and clubs.

Big developments had occurred since Hurricane Katrina. Probably the hurricane was the catalyst for change.

You will recall that the hurricane struck in August 2005. A huge area was flooded by up to fifteen feet of water. 80% of New Orleans and large tracts of neighbouring parishes were covered; and the flood waters lingered for weeks. About 2000 people lost their lives, half of them in and around New Orleans.

It could have marked the end of jazz in the city; and indeed the homes of many musicians were destroyed and they had to leave.

But from 2006, as the City started to rebuild, a new young generation began to migrate to New Orleans. They came from all parts of America, as well as a few from Canada, Japan and Europe. They were mostly young white musicians - some of them fresh out of music colleges - and they started to settle in New Orleans in the hope of making a career in music. Surprisingly, many of them wanted to play the good old tunes (of 1910 - 1940) in the original styles. Learning from 78 rpm records, and CD reissues and increasingly from the internet (especially YouTube) they mastered music that had rarely been played in the previous 70 years.

It was a hard life and I guess some of them soon gave up. But many settled. They made just enough money to survive by playing for tips on the streets. They started to find like-minded musicians who became their friends and they formed themselves into bands. The best example was *The Loose Marbles* - a band in which founder members were Ben Polcer (a graduate of the University of Michigan) and Michael Magro. They encouraged promising newcomers to pass through the band's ranks and hone their skills. Many of the musicians who developed their talents in *Loose Marbles* have gone on to form bands of their own: think not only of Tuba Skinny, but also of *Tom Saunders and the Tom Cats*, *Meschiya Lake and the Little Big Horns*, and *The Orleans Six*, for example.

Shaye Cohn said: 'One thing really important to *The Loose Marbles* was ensemble playing. When I first started with them, I was playing second trumpet. So I had to work to find a voice where I could fit in. It taught me to play very simply, and to listen'.

The Loose Marbles still exists and is attracting plenty of gigs. As the sixty or so musicians who have played in *Loose Marbles* all still feel part of the family, it is easy enough for Ben and Michael to put together half a dozen of them to play at a gig.

To see a video of great historical interest - The Loose Marbles playing in the street in 2007, go on YouTube and type in 'Meschiya Lake and the Loose Marbles - Coconut Island' (It's https://www.youtube.com/watch?v=-kND3dzwR0w#t=152). And to see them playing indoors in those early post-Katrina days, type in 'Loose Marbles at Donna's' (https://www.youtube.com/watch?v=q8TU_OSHm7c#t=35)

The great banjo player John Dixon (of The Shotgun Jazz Band – also based in New Orleans) told me that with the musicians came some great dancers - people such as Amy Johnson and Chance Bushman; and they in turn attracted more dancers..... and so more musicians.

In the hottest months, it became customary to decamp to the cooler regions in the north, so you might find these bands in August busking in New York's Washington Square, for example. Some of the musicians headed north in August to work as tutors in residential Jazz Camps. More recently, some of the bands have even been able to tour overseas during the summer.

As part of their learning and development, some players, after arriving in New Orleans, decided to take up a second or even a third instrument. They taught themselves and - in just a few years - reached the highest levels on these instruments. Think of Barnabus Jones. He arrived in New Orleans as a violinist. He then mastered the banjo. And finally he bought an old trombone and went on to be regarded as one of the finest traditional jazz trombonists in the history of jazz. Then there is Shaye Cohn. She arrived as an outstanding pianist and accomplished violinist. She obtained a very old cornet (which she still plays - she told me in 2015 it was the only horn she possessed), taught herself the fingering, and just a few years later had surely become the most creative traditional jazz cornet player in the world.

Todd Burdick arrived in New Orleans as a banjo and guitar player. He is now one of the best jazz tuba players. And that wasn't enough. He went on to learn to play the string bass to add to his armoury. Todd told me with some regret he hardly ever gets invited to play a gig on banjo these days because 'people seem to have forgotten that I play the instrument'!

As the years have gone by, bands have emerged and developed - all with distinctive styles. Hundreds of hours spent making music on the streets and later playing at gigs in bars and clubs have brought the standard of traditional jazz performance in New Orleans to a musical level at least equal to that of the 1920s.

The boom in tourism and the world-wide appreciation of their music (fostered by YouTube, internet-streamed performances and CDs) has meant that the best bands no longer need to play on the streets to make a living. They can survive on the income from gigs mainly in the bars and clubs on Frenchmen Street. Indeed, Frenchmen Street is the place to be - though the great tradition still continues at Preservation Hall: every night, whenever I have been in town, there has been a long queue in St. Peter's Street waiting for the Hall to open.

Some of the best bands to emerge since Katrina have practically given up busking in the streets, because it is such hard work and it has become so difficult to secure a prime spot. But others (including Tuba Skinny) still choose to play in the streets at least once a week because they see this as a chance to try out new ideas and to spread the music to the people. They say it is good to play what you like when you like, without any pressures from a promoter. Incidentally, the acoustics are much better in the street than in the bars so the public gets to hear the instruments really well.

Meanwhile, more young musicians have gone on arriving in New Orleans to try their luck. The most outstanding (such as James Evans from Wales and Haruka Kikuchi from Japan) have rapidly been recruited into established bands.

On the streets the musicians playing for tips have continued to multiply. In my view, there are now too many for their own good, because competition has made it hard to earn a living. Even so, I have to report the standards of the music to be heard on Royal Street are so high that those bands are much better and more exciting than the typical band that we find in pubs and jazz clubs here in England.

These words from guitarist Shine Delphi show just how hard they work - even on a birthday:
Thank y'all for the birthday love. If you're in New Orleans come give me a hug. I'll be busking with Yes Ma'am 11 - 2, then Goorin Bros hat shop 3 - 5 and I'll finish the evening over at Buffa's 11 - 1.

While I was in New Orleans I had the privilege of conversations with several of the musicians I had previously seen and admired only on YouTube. It was a special thrill to meet them. I learned a great deal about their approach to the music, and how they practise, rehearse and manage their lives.

TUBA SKINNY AT HOME IN NOLA

During my visit to New Orleans in April 2015, I had for the first time the pleasure of hearing in person the wonderful young band. I attended three of their performances.

On one occasion the band comprised Craig Flory, Shaye Cohn, Barnabus Jones, Erika Lewis, Todd Burdick, Jason Lawrence, Max Bien-Kahn and Robin Rapuzzi. At other performances they had Charlie Halloran on trombone and Jonathan Doyle on reeds.

I was specially pleased to see Max Bien-Kahn playing regularly with the band (Greg Sherman had departed to the north) as I have always admired Max's strong, solid, concentrated performances on YouTube, and I don't think he has had the recognition he deserves.

A bonus was that I was able to have a chat with some of the players.

Todd Burdick (Mr. Tuba Skinny himself) is best known as the Bb tuba player and a founder member. After Hurricane Katrina, he was among the many young musicians who migrated to New Orleans. Todd moved there from Chicago and he told me that at the time you could find a pal and jointly rent a shotgun house near the French Quarter for just 400 dollars a month. (The price by 2017 had risen to 950 dollars a month.)

From Todd Burdick and Robin Rapuzzi (washboard), I learned a good deal about Tuba Skinny. By the way, Robin told me that as an infant he had occasionally visited Nottingham to stay with his grandmother. This appealed to me as Nottingham is where I live and am writing right now.

I had often wondered how Tuba Skinny go about unearthing the obscure tunes from the 1920s and 1930s that now form a substantial part of their repertoire. Todd pointed out that it's no longer necessary for someone to have a vintage 78rpm recording. Today there is so much available, not only on re-issued CDs but even on the internet - especially YouTube. For example, the band introduced *Dear Almanzoer* into its repertoire in 2014. This is a lively composition by Oscar 'Papa' Celestin and was recorded in 1927 by his band. Thanks to the kindness of various YouTube uploaders, Todd said, you can freely listen to - and learn from - the Celestin original.

I had wondered whether the members of Tuba Skinny get together for private rehearsals occasionally. After all, some of their music is tricky, with complicated arrangements. Think of *Cannonball Blues* as a typical example: with so many surprising key changes and various ensemble phrasing patterns to remember, you can't just turn up and play such a tune. Everybody needs to have learned exactly what their rôle is at any given point. Robin told me much of the experimenting and 'rehearsing' takes place on the street. They liked to play in Royal Street every week if possible. But they did also have an occasional private rehearsal in one of their houses, perhaps once a month. They had recently been rehearsing once a week - but this was in the lead-up to the recording of their seventh CD - Blue Chime Stomp. The recording took place over two days in early April 2015.

They told me they guessed *The Smoking Time Jazz Club Band* - similar in some ways to themselves, but continually playing even more complicated arrangements - surely gets together to rehearse more frequently.

I asked about the 'arranging' of the more complex of Tuba Skinny's tunes. It seems obvious that Shaye Cohn is the expert in this matter and has a big say (though she modestly claimed she does not need to do much other than 'direct the traffic' in performance). I was assured that the band's decisions are 'democratic' and that all contribute ideas, though it's a fact that Shaye will sometimes supply a 'chart', especially for banjo and guitar players.

I mentioned *Maple Leaf Rag* as an example. It had been recently introduced into Tuba Skinny's repertoire and obviously they had to decide in which key to play it (some bands go for Eb moving into Ab; but Tuba Skinny chose F going into Bb). They also had to make up their minds about which of the tune's four possible melodic themes they should play and in which order, and whether with any distinctive treatments. And they had to decide whether to include an introduction, bridges and a coda. If you type in 'Tuba Skinny - Maple Leaf Rag' (https://www.youtube.com/watch?v=kYJhgz4L3UU), you will see what they came up with. Enjoy especially the use of those long harmonising notes in the final choruses preceding the out-chorus. When they played *Maple Leaf Rag* at The French Quarter Festival a few weeks later, with slightly different personnel, the arrangement was essentially the same, though with two fewer of the 16-bar final choruses, and also this time there was a two-bar coda - I guess a spur-of-the-moment Shaye-ism that took nobody by surprise! Enjoy it by typing in Tuba Skinny 'Maple Leaf Rag FQF 4/12/15' (https://www.youtube.com/watch?v=9OdJvQQOxV8).

Todd told me he had recently deputised in another band which had also played *Maple Leaf Rag*. But their version turned out to be quite different from Tuba Skinny's. Did this cause him any difficulty? Not really. He easily picked up what was going on.

I was gratified when Erika Lewis told me that, when the band was planning a play-list, they would sometimes consult my list of their tunes (published in my Blog called 'Enjoying

Traditional Jazz') to remind themselves of titles they hadn't performed recently and that perhaps ought to be revived. So I had become the honorary archivist to the band! (You can consult that list of tunes at the end of this book.)

The first time I saw Tuba Skinny in person, they were playing in a very crowded bar. I assumed the great number of people had all gone there specially to hear the band. I was wrong. I was trapped in the middle of the crowd near the bar, unable to move and quite a few yards from the stage. When the band started to play, I found the din of conversation around me was so loud that I could hardly hear the music. And so it continued. I felt so disappointed for the musicians, even more than for myself: they were producing such wonderful music and yet only a few people near the stage could hear them clearly.

When I eventually met Shaye, I told her how sorry I was that the band had been treated in this way. She shrugged her shoulders philosophically and said, 'Well, it's a bar....'.

But no wonder the band still so much enjoys playing in the street, where they can be clearly heard and be given respect by people who love their music.

I had constantly wondered how Shaye manages to create all those wonderful phrases she plays (often with a mute) as a backing to Erika's vocals and also in support when the trombone or clarinet takes the melody. I asked her whether, while playing, she was thinking her way through the chords. She paused to consider my question for a moment, as if she had never thought about the process before. Yes, she knew the chords all right; but she felt that her inventions had become 'intuitive'.

In chatting with Barnabus, I got on to the unlikely topic of diminished chords. When I hummed a particularly enjoyable phrase he had played over a diminished chord in a YouTube video some years earlier, he remembered exactly the one I meant and said he had picked the phrase up from Ewan Bleach!

One evening I bumped into that brilliant and ubiquitous trombonist Charlie Halloran. When he told me he would be playing with Tuba Skinny the following night (deputising during an absence of Barnabus Jones), I asked him how he would cope with Tuba Skinny's often complex head arrangements. What if they played *Deep Henderson*, for example? He said *Deep Henderson* would be no trouble, as he knew their arrangement well. However, he told me 'I expect they will dumb down the programme a bit to make allowances for me.'

Well, I went to the concert. And I can tell you this: Tuba Skinny did not 'dumb down' at all. They played a typical programme, complex arrangements included. And how did Charlie cope? Brilliantly. He played some wonderful stuff and, as far as I could tell, never put a foot wrong. I discovered later that Charlie plays so often with Tuba Skinny that he is clearly well versed in their repertoire.

I enjoyed observing how Shaye prepares a playlist. At The French Quarter Festival, for a quarter hour before the performance started, she sat in her place looking at her notebooks and working out a programme. She wrote the tune titles in large lettering on a sheet of paper which she then placed on the floor in the centre of the band, so that all members could know what was coming next. I noticed how skilfully she made the programme entertaining by alternating slower and quicker tunes, and mixing instrumental with vocal numbers, and even ensuring a variety of keys.

Watching Tuba Skinny perform their specials - such as *Freight Train Blues* and the new ones by Shaye - *Tangled Blues* and *Blue Chime Stomp* - it was such a joy to observe at close quarters how brilliant they all are, and such perfectionists.

SHAYE COHN

Shaye Cohn used to play a pocket trumpet before obtaining a cornet. You can find her busking powerfully and joyfully on a pocket trumpet in videos dating from 2008.

But today her kit consists of a long-model cornet that is surely older than Shaye herself. Its plating is worn round some of the tubes and valves, suggesting that it has had heavy use for many years. What a museum-piece it is!

A correspondent told me it was made by Yamaha. To me it looks like a YCR-234 from the 1970s. It's the kind of cornet you could pick up on an Internet auction for about 100 dollars.

Bob Andersen of San Diego has kindly emailed me to say Shaye's cornet formerly belonged to Ed Polcer, father of the very fine New Orleans jazz trumpeter Ben Polcer. Ed had been playing jazz cornet for 55 years!

Shaye also loves her Humes and Berg 102 stone-lined cup mute. With this, Shaye achieves the most glorious, crisp jazzy effects.

The same is true of the other mutes - the black rubber plunger and the amazing battered piece of metal that she used to use – a terrific sound-modifier. Bob Andersen told me it was simply an 'aluminum canning funnel'!

Finally - proof that Shaye likes to keep the cornet in good condition with freely-moving valves – she carries a tube of Al Cass 'Fast' oil from Massachusetts, which is held in high regard by brass players. You can see Shaye using it to lubricate a sticky third-valve piston (at 1 min. 50 secs.) in a video accessible by typing 'Tuba Skinny @ Louisiana Music Factory Grand Opening Celebration on Frenchmen St. 2014

PT1' in YouTube (https://www.youtube.com/watch?v=-ErCBXGrPQ4).

Yet, with this modest kit (total value about 180 U.S. dollars) Shaye produces some of the most sublime traditional jazz to be heard in the world today. There could be no better proof that a really great performer can strut his or her stuff without recourse to expensive equipment.

Shaye is not an exhibitionist. Not from her will you hear those screaming, raucous, high-note 32-bar solo choruses to which so many traditional jazz trumpeters resort.

But she is a very energetic player of the cornet. She produces a unique tone that perfectly encapsulates the blues feeling that is at the heart of so much of our music. Listen closely to her busy fluent phrases, often muted and in the background, interwoven brilliantly into the polyphony of her band's wonderful music. As I have said, her contributions to ensembles remind me of the viola parts in Mozart's string quartets. (She is also great at what Punch Miller used to call 'fast fingering'.)

Shaye has an instinctive understanding of rhythmic possibilities, subtle and surprising harmonies and progressions, even when improvising at high speed. She can 'bend' notes to great effect and in exactly the right places.

She always works hard to encourage great teamwork from the *band*, not just to display her own skills. Her playing takes account of (and usually directs) all that is going on around her.

In fact, she seems to be the principal arranger of the music for Tuba Skinny - discovering long-forgotten gems from recordings made by jazz bands and string bands and jug-blower bands 80 - 90 years ago, and making them sound completely fresh and exciting, with all the armoury of breaks, stop chords, sustained notes, offbeat rhythms, clever introductions and codas, key changes and so on. Shaye holds all this in her head for an astonishingly wide repertoire of tunes.

Shaye also takes great care in setting tempos before a tune is started. And when a fast tempo is required, she and the band ensure it is maintained with excitement and no dragging later in the tune.

On top of all this, Shaye is a fine composer of tunes for traditional jazz bands. On YouTube you can witness performances by Tuba Skinny of *Blue Chime Stomp*, *Nigel's Dream*, *Owl Call Blues*, *Pyramid Strut*, *Salamanca Blues*, *Deep Bayou Moan* and *Tangled Blues* - all of them fine pieces of music composed by Shaye for the band.

And that is not all. Shaye is also one of the best traditional jazz *pianists*! You can enjoy evidence of this by typing Tuba Skinny - Orvieto 29 dicembre 2013 and so getting to the video https://www.youtube.com/watch?v=3kMeQ68cpus.

Elsewhere on YouTube, you will find her contributing lustily on piano in a 'country' music group, playing some cowboy-style music.

And Shaye's talents do not end there: she may also be heard and seen on YouTube playing the violin and the accordion (and even the spoons!) very well indeed. In 2016, she even took up playing the trombone - and formed an all-female band that she called *The Shake 'Em Up Jazz Band*.

Shaye's grandfather was Alvin Cohn, who was a tenor saxophone player, composer and arranger, including for the

Woody Herman band. He died in 1988. Her father Joe Cohn studied at the Berklee College of Music and is a well-known jazz guitarist. It is often said that Shaye inherited her talents from her father and grandfather. There may be some truth in this, though I am sure Shaye has worked extremely hard to develop her own skills and versatility and to play the music in her own way. I also believe greater credit should be given to her mother Yas Ishibashi - a very fine jazz pianist and singer who, in my opinion, may have had an even deeper influence on Shaye.

Shaye is a very happy person, often to be seen smiling or laughing. But she is also very serious about her work. She strives so hard to get the best possible sounds both from her own playing and from her bands. She expresses herself through her music and never in the publicity-seeking ways of many stars in the entertainment world. She seems unaware of her own greatness and of the huge admiration she has won from people all over the world. Shaye is a very private person and, I suspect, even rather shy.

And what about that distinctive tone she achieves with her cornet? It is impossible to put into words the quality of a sound. We can only do our best.

So let me say first that most cornet players aim to produce a beautifully clean, clear, open, round, full tone. Think of the best English brass bands. (By the way, brass bands in England - those who participate in national contests and who perform in park bandstands during the summer - are quite different from the jazz 'brass bands' that you find in New Orleans.) The cornet players of such bands as Black Dyke, Brighouse and Rastrick, Foden's and Cory are examples of players who achieve this angelic purity of tone.

But traditional jazz cornet (and trumpet) players need a tone that is a little bit rougher and that allows for jazzy effects - bending notes, being bluesy and occasionally even rasping a little. Very few of them have much use for that sublime purity of tone common among the top English-style brass band players.

And Shaye Cohn - possibly the best and certainly the most interesting traditional jazz cornet player to be heard today - has succeeded in developing a tone that is perfect for her 1920s style of music. It is distinctive and unique. I can't think of any other cornet player who sounds or has sounded like her. At best, I can say her tone is midway between those of George Mitchell (1899 - 1972) and Natty Dominique (1896 - 1982).

She picks up that very old Yamaha cornet and off she goes - always producing an amazing tone that is immediately recognizable and that is such an essential ingredient in the success of Tuba Skinny. The remarkable tone is always distinctive, no matter how fast, or athletic, or creative the musical phrases she produces.

How does she achieve it? I doubt whether even Shaye knows. It must have something to do with the physiology of her mouth and the way she uses her lips. I guess it is instinctive rather than cultivated.

She loves her mutes - especially the plunger and the Humes and Berg 102 stone-lined cup mutes; and she uses these for tonal effects. She particularly enjoys holding them only partially inside the bell of the instrument.

But these alone do not account for her special tone. Observe her even when she is playing without a mute: the sound is still peculiarly her own.

If you are a cornet player and think you can produce a sound exactly like Shaye Cohn's, well - just try! I doubt whether you will get anywhere near it.

This tone, combined with the creativity, energy and subtlety she puts into all her playing, makes Shaye the outstanding traditional jazz musician of her generation (not to mention that - as I have said - she also pays brilliantly on several other instruments - notably the piano and violin).

If by any chance you are still discovering Shaye, I can tell you there are plenty more videos in which you can witness her wonderful playing for yourself.

For example, try this - 'Tuba Skinny - Deep Henderson - Rapperswil 30 juni 2013'
(to be found at https://www.youtube.com/watch?v=qqVx9vwt2WM).

And probably the most amazing thing about Shaye's cornet playing is that she did not even begin learning to play the instrument until she settled in New Orleans after Hurricane Katrina. Following her classical music training, she arrived in New Orleans as a player of the piano, accordion and violin.

Type in 'Mucca Pazza @ Empty Bottle, Chicago 06/02/07' to watch a video of Shaye playing accordion with the phenomenal Mucca Pazza Band in the days when she was about 24 years old and before she moved to New Orleans.

SHAYE'S MOZARTIAN QUALITIES

Shaye Cohn's playing reminds me of Mozart. In particular, it makes me think of the viola part in Mozart's string quartets.

Here's why. Mozart's quartets are like lively interesting well-informed conversations between four intelligent and sympathetic friends. If you study the viola's rôle in a Mozart string quartet, what do you discover?

The viola sometimes takes the lead (playing the melody, you could say) but more often you find it responding, commenting cleverly and perceptively on the remarks of the others, coming up with surprising original thoughts, sparkling and witty, or sad, sympathetic and pensive as the occasion demands. It can play very quickly, producing a lot of notes rapidly when there is something exciting to say. But the viola does not show off or attempt to dominate. It both compli*m*ents and compl*e*ments the contributions of the other instruments.

Shaye's playing in any jazz ensemble is exactly like that. She is not a showy player. One of my Blog readers emailed me to say he watches her solos 'with anticipation. What comes next? Her playing is so unpredictable'. I know exactly what he means. The rest of us can play cliché-ridden improvisations but Shaye seems effortlessly to come up with phrases that are magical and stunning in their originality.

Most of us agree she is probably the best and most creative traditional jazz cornet player in the world today and yet she opts for subtle, inventive musical phrases that rarely go above the stave. In fact, having listened to her in about 450 videos, I have never heard her play a note higher than Concert A above the stave. Music theorists call it 'A5', equivalent to vibrations at 880 times per second (880 Hz). You can hear Shaye using this note when playing *Dallas Rag*.

She is an example to us all. There are trumpeters who can frequently be heard squeezing out notes at 1046 Hz (the note called 'C5') and even higher. But what's the point?

She is so energetic in her playing and her thinking. One of my friends - Lou in the USA - has twice sent me emails in praise of Shaye; and they are worth quoting:
I find myself more and more separating her horn from the rest of the piece. I've discovered that she has a very versatile tongue. One just knows that she doesn't have to think about what's coming next for her. She may think ahead for the arrangement, but her playing just flows naturally. I can hear the little notes she drops here and there that she just has to do because they belong.
and:
I marvel at her stamina in numbers like 'Weary Blues'. She just blows her heart out, all in such a matter of fact way.
I think Lou is absolutely right.

Listen closely to her busy fluent phrases, often muted and in the background, interwoven brilliantly into the polyphony of her band's wonderful music. That's why I am reminded of the viola in Mozart's string quartets. I have to say I have not come across a traditional jazz musician who impresses me more than Shaye. She is simply the best.

SHAYE THE COMPOSER

Shaye Cohn is considered by many to be the best traditional jazz band leader, the best traditional jazz cornet player and one of the best traditional jazz piano players and violin players in the world today. I think it's time also for us to recognise her achievement as a *composer* of our kind of music.

While only in her early 30s, Shaye had already given us some wonderful compositions. Think of the very entertaining and clever *Blue Chime Stomp*. Remember the haunting *Owl Call Blues*. And there was *Salamanca Blues* - a lovely melancholy piece with themes in F and then Ab, giving plenty of opportunities to the trombone and banjo. The medium-tempo *Tangled Blues* is a particularly clever composition: as its title suggests, it sets us plenty to 'untangle', with pretty, wistful phrases popping up in different keys and in two different themes - one of which runs for the highly unusual length of 18 bars. Then there is the mighty Mortonesque *Pyramid Strut*, composed while the band Tuba Skinny was touring in Australia. This is the most complex of Shaye's creations. It has four themes, as well as an 8-bar bridge, and uses two keys. Lots of 'breaks' are built in and there are witty moments - such as the Coda. You can find videos of all these tunes on YouTube.

Shaye's composition *Nigel's Dream* sounds so authentically 1920s that you could easily be fooled into thinking it was a previously undiscovered manuscript by King Oliver.

You can hear Shaye and Tuba Skinny performing *Nigel's Dream* either at https://www.youtube.com/watch?v=p1-vc0YVodU or at https://www.youtube.com/watch?v=-mH63AsRRuw. As ever, we must be grateful to the videomakers (in this case *James Sterling* and *RaoulDuke504*) for bringing this tune to our attention.

Its cheeky two-bar introduction involves nothing more than one 'Charleston' bar from the washboard followed by a single chord from the banjo, guitar and tuba. Then we are into Theme A - 32 bars in the key of C. Great use is made of a phrase (reminiscent of the Middle Eight of *East Coast Trot*) in which a flattened third is accentuated. Actually these 32 bars comprise two almost identical 16s; and at the end of the first sixteen (Bars 15 and 16) we have a 'break' (played by the banjo first time through and by the cornet and clarinet in a witty King Oliver-style mini-duet when the Theme is played again, led by the trombone, later).

The final bar of Theme A takes us through a modulating chord into the Key of Eb, in which Theme B is played. Twice through the sixteen bars (apparently both beginning with the chord sequence IV - IV - I - I) gives us a merry 32 bars. We then go straight back into Theme A (key of C again), with the trombone taking the lead. Then Theme B (in Eb) is re-visited. This is played through a couple of times with some boisterous, polyphonic ensemble, giving the piece a great ending. There is a neat Coda of just one bar.

What a composition! It's just as well written and well played as those King Oliver Jazz Band classics from the 1920s.

SHAYE AS PERFORMANCE DIRECTOR

What a performance!

The tune is Fats Waller's *Minor Drag*. Listen to it but hold on to your hats! Note all the subtle signals Shaye gives by means of eye contact, body language, quick words to John Doyle (clarinet) and Barnabus (trombone), a hand signal to Robin (washboard), the notes she holds at the ends of choruses - even left hand on the head to signal a return to Theme A!

It would be hard to find a better example than this video of a leader carefully setting the right tempo, driving the band along, directing the musical traffic and making very clear what is wanted from everyone, while working up some great excitement in the music.

Type into YouTube 'Tuba Skinny - Minor drag - Rapperswil 30 juni 2013'. This should take you to https://www.youtube.com/watch?v=J_jB_WbPg9I.

Incidentally, why on earth don't more bands follow Tuba Skinny's example in seating arrangements? Having the band in an arc means the audience can see all the musicians and - for signalling purposes - the musicians can all see each other.

In other videos, you can even see Shaye 'conducting' the band by extending a bare foot! She does so near the end to indicate that this is to be the final chorus.

SETTING THE TEMPO

Listening to bands in pubs and clubs, and watching videos of performances on YouTube, I have noticed that so many bands have difficulty with setting and keeping to a suitable tempo.

The worst problem (very common) is that bands start an up-tempo tune quickly and then, as the performance develops, gradually slow down. The result is that the music begins to drag and sound weary. I think the reason for this may partly be that so many musicians are growing old and have lost the vigour they once had. But I wish they would be aware of this and take more care.

The reverse sometimes happens: a tune speeds up as it is played. This can put one or two of the players (as well as a singer) into difficulties.

However, speeding up is by no means as bad as slowing down and can even be deliberate and exciting, especially if building to a special 'out' chorus. The Ken Colyer Band used to be noted for this and they themselves described it as 'controlled acceleration'.

With slower tunes, such as many ballads, there is less of a problem, though I sometimes find bands take a tune *too* slowly and it begins to drag.

When there is a singer, it is important that the tempo should be one the singer is comfortable with, so it helps to ask the singer to give an indication of the tempo desired or even to count the song in.

As in so many aspects of traditional jazz performance, Tuba Skinny are setting an example to us all. Notice how much trouble they take to get the tempo right. This is often done with much foot-tapping before the tune begins, while they (especially Shaye) test the tune inside their heads just before starting; and they always keep the tempo under control throughout the performance, with rigid discipline from the rhythm section.

This aspect of their playing rewards study. For a typical example (and a good tune - *Deep Henderson*), try the YouTube video 'Tuba Skinny - Deep Henderson - Rapperswil 30 juni 2013' (https://www.youtube.com/watch?v=qqVx9vwt2WM).

TODD AND BARNABUS

Lou, an elderly American friend, has corresponded with me from time to time and recently sent this message, which I think ought to be shared.

I have commented on a few members of Tuba Skinny, but I have to mention Barnabus. Of course I listened to the traditional recorded dixieland growing up. But we spent every weekend during my college days at a local jazz place. We listened to the 'Dixiecrats', a great band consisting of piano, tenor sax, trumpet, clarinet, string bass and drums. The tenor and sax played with Cab Calloway and the clarinet played with Louis Armstrong in the early days in NOLA. So I was pretty used to a band without a trombone, and never gave the instrument much thought. As a matter of fact, we thought of our taste in dixieland as rather elite....no tuba, no banjo, strictly 'Chicago Style'.
Tuba Skinny has totally changed my thinking on the subject, which is a lengthy lead-in to Barnabus.
I suspect that he, Shaye and Todd go back to their earliest days together and that they have not only a strong personal relationship, but are attuned to one another musically. Barnabus is such a strong player. He's always where he should be, whether it's lead or support. I still find it hard to believe that he just picked up a horn and taught himself. He certainly plays like he has a deep musical background. The same thing seems true of Todd. He's so gentle that at times he sounds like a string bass, and he's so important as part of TS's rhythm section.
Have I pontificated enough?
Regards,
Lou

I am so pleased Lou paid this tribute to Barnabus and Todd. Tuba Skinny fans (including myself) are so seduced by the amazing talents of the ladies - Shaye and Erika - that we don't give sufficient credit to the other players - especially Todd, who goes unnoticed by most people while never putting a foot wrong in the 'engine room' of the band.

Sometimes, when listening to a tune played by Tuba Skinny, I deliberately focus my attention on ONE instrument. It is a great way to appreciate the magic of this band. I am invariably amazed at how that one instrument contributes to the overall structure. In the case of Barnabus, Lou is so right about his strengths, whether leading on the melody or supporting other players. And Todd has an uncanny ability to find the perfect bass line, no matter how complicated the piece. Maybe the fact that both these men are also banjo players - and therefore understand chord sequences - helps a little. What great musicians they both are!

BARNABUS AND GLISSANDI

One of the special effects that any trombonist can contribute to a performance by a traditional jazz band is the glissando, where he uses his slide to move (sometimes down but more often up) from one note to another. Most commonly, it is used on the last beat of a bar, dragging up to the first beat of the next bar, and in the process moving either the melody or the chord progression or both on to the next change.

So let me tell you about an amazing use of trombone glissandos. The trombonist is Barnabus on Tuba Skinny's CD called 'Rag Band'.

In the song *I'd Rather Drink Muddy Water* (a 12-bar blues from 1936 performed in the key of G), Barnabus plays *nothing but* glissandos. There are - I think - 96 bars (i.e. eight choruses) - not counting the Introduction - and Barnabus plays a glissando leading into *every* odd-numbered bar. So he plays 48 glissandos in all. AND ABSOLUTELY NOTHING ELSE! He begins every glissando on the 4th beat of a bar, slides up to the required note by the first beat of the next bar and then sustains the note for several beats, thereby underpinning all that is going on in the rest of the band.

I don't know whose idea this was. Maybe they simply decided to have a bit of fun, to see how it would work.

The answer is that it works amazingly well. Whether accompanying Erika's singing, or Shaye's piano chorus, or the clarinet solo, the glissandos are unrelenting; and they are very effective in pumping the tune along.

What a *tour de force*!

You can listen to the performance by going to:
https://tubaskinny.bandcamp.com/album/rag-band

Then click on the second tune. You will be allowed to hear it - free. But maybe you will also consider helping this wonderful band by buying the CD. You can do this online: just follow the instructions on the page. I have done it; and it works easily and well.

BARNABUS SINGS

I enjoyed listening to Tuba Skinny on YouTube performing a fun song called *Do It Right* (not to be confused with other songs of the same name). Barnabus leads the community singing. Here is the performance: http://www.youtube.com/watch?v=lEyDV0eb47E.

Or you can access it by typing in 'Tuba Skinny at Bearsville Theater Do It Right'.

My friend Peter Killeen kindly informed me this song (composed by someone credited only as 'Jones') was recorded (Columbia 14463) in 1929 by Pigmeat Pete and Catjuice Charlie (pseudonyms of Wesley Wilson and Harry McDaniels). Possibly 'Jones' was a pseudonym of Wesley Wilson, who wrote many songs, together with his wife. This was an Age of Pseudonyms: as a double act, the married couple worked under various names. To hear the original Columbia recording on YouTube, type in 'Do It Right ~ Pigmeat Pete and Catjuice Charlie'.

It is essentially a typical 12-bar of the 1920s. It's easy to pick up if you would care to add it to your band's repertoire and the words are very clear in that original Columbia recording.

ROBIN RAPUZZI

During my April 2016 visit to New Orleans, I had the great pleasure of again meeting the percussionist of Tuba Skinny, Robin Rapuzzi. I had met him for the first time during the French Quarter Festival of 2015, when we had some conversations that I enjoyed and from which I learned a lot.

Before he became a celebrated washboard player, Robin was a full-kit percussionist. He played the drum set at a young age and this led to participating in punk rock bands at high school. At that time, he also learned the guitar and harmonica. He enjoyed playing sea shanties, Woodie Guthrie tunes, and compositions of his own. He considered himself a 'folk musician' up to the time when he moved to New Orleans, where he took up the washboard specialism, joined Tuba Skinny and...... the rest is history.

On some occasions, he told me, he felt a bit limited in using the washboard only. For example, for such a tune as *New Orleans Bump*, he said that with the snare and Chinese tom-drum and china-crash cymbal he could access the depth and true texture that such a 'stompy' number deserved.

Since early 2015, he has returned to playing a full percussion set even in the streets. How has he managed to transport so much kit? The answer is that he hauls it around in a trailer attached to his bicycle. (He calls pedalling this load into the French Quarter his 'daily work-out'!)

Most of the New Orleans musicians use bicycles: it's almost impossible to park a car in the French Quarter.

I also had the very great pleasure this year of meeting Robin's lovely wife, Magda. She is Polish and is a highly-talented artist: she has produced some amazing and distinctive work, often of dwellings in New Orleans but also sometimes combining mythical animal and human images with tremendous attention to detail. Her silk-screen prints are sold at The Foundation Gallery in Royal Street and the Hall-Barnett Gallery on Chartres, as well as in other galleries.

I realised a few days after meeting her that I had long admired Magda's work (through the internet) before discovering that she was married to Robin.

Although most fans think of Robin as a member of Tuba Skinny, he actually performs in several bands. He clearly enjoys the variety of work and is proud of them all. I think he was particularly pleased that I turned up to hear him with The Rhythm Wizards; and I made a video of them playing *Ice Cream*, in which you can see Robin at work in close-up. View it by typing into YouTube 'The Rhythm Wizards: Ice Cream'. I also filmed them playing *Cotton-Picker's Drag*. You can watch that performance by typing 'The Rhythm Wizards : Cotton-Picker's Drag'. I'm afraid the sound isn't exactly perfect (my fault for walking round while they were playing) but I think this video gives a genuine feel for what it is like to be a member of a street band in New Orleans.

On another day, I found Robin playing with The Hokum High Rollers. I made a video of them playing *Michigander Blues*. You may watch it by typing 'The Hokum High Rollers: 'Michigander Blues'.

There are hundreds of videos on YouTube of Robin playing with Tuba Skinny. But if you would like to watch the one I made of them playing *Hilarity Rag* during this April 2016 visit, type 'Tuba Skinny : 'Hilarity Rag'. This is of historic interest because Robin told me it was a tune the Band had only just learned and this was its first public performance.

Robin was in England during June 2016 and again touring in Europe in the summer of 2017. (His mother is English.) He teamed up with his friend Ewan Bleach - the great English reed player (not to mention pianist and singer) who worked in New Orleans with Tuba Skinny for several months.

One of the interesting things Robin also told me is that it's not just the fans who enjoy the YouTube videos. He said many musicians - including himself - use them as learning tools. They analyse their own performances and consider what improvements could be made. He found it particularly interesting to spot how his own backing of, say, trombone solo choruses varied according to which trombonist he was playing with.

I think there's a message for us all: we should not just enjoy videos but also use them as tools for analysing and improving playing.

CHARLIE HALLORAN

One of the hardest-working and most versatile of the hugely-talented musicians I met during my visit to New Orleans in April 2015 was the trombone player Charlie Halloran. Charlie is one of the many young players who migrated to New Orleans - in his case from St. Louis - shortly after Hurricane Katrina.

Charlie had earlier studied at Webster University and went on to the Eastman School of Music in Rochester, New York.

It is not surprising that Charlie is in great demand. Is there any tune in any style that he can't play brilliantly? It seems not. I should mention that he's a pretty good singer, too.

During the four days of the official French Quarter Festival he played in at least nine concerts featuring various contrasting bands - *The Palmetto Bug Stompers*, *Tom Saunders and the Tomcats*, *Diablo's Horns*, *The Panorama Jazz Band*, *Steve Pistorius's Southern Syncopators*, *Cori Walters and the Universe Jazz Band*, *Orange Kellin's New Orleans Deluxe Orchestra*, and *Tim Laughlin's Band*. On top of these official Festival engagements, I saw him twice - in the evenings - playing with *The Shotgun Jazz Band* and with Tuba Skinny.

All that in four days. What stamina! What energy!

Charlie approaches his music in the same way as a great athlete approaches competition. He always aims to get a good sleep and does not stay out late when he doesn't have to. He makes a point of eating well.

Even on a day when there will be a lot of playing, he aims to be up by 9am to spend some time practising the trombone -

'warming up carefully' and 'playing long tones'. He carries in his kit a gel that he can apply to his lips in case of emergency. He says this helps prevent his lips from becoming swollen later in the day. (I noticed that Haruka Kikuchi, another great trombonist, frequently applies vaseline to her lips during a performance.)

Yet, despite his massive talent, Charlie is such a modest and gentlemanly person, always friendly and willing to chat during his few spare moments. He loves his work but enjoys being a side-man rather a leader or star. When he told me he would be playing with Tuba Skinny the following night (deputising during an absence of Barnabus Jones), I asked him how he would cope with Tuba Skinny's often complex head arrangements. What if they played *Deep Henderson*, for example? He said *Deep Henderson* would be no trouble, as he knew their arrangement well. However, he told me 'I expect they will dumb down the programme a bit to make allowances for me.'

Well, I went to the concert. And I can tell you this: Tuba Skinny did not 'dumb down' at all. They played a typical programme, complex arrangements included. And how did Charlie cope? Brilliantly. He played some wonderful stuff and, as far as I could tell, never put a foot wrong.

Listen to Charlie for yourself:

In this video, Charlie talks to us and gives a demonstration of some styles: Type in YouTube 'Welbourne Jazz Camp 2013 - Meet Charlie Halloran'.
And listen to a lovely gentle tune in 3/4 time with *The Panorama Jazz Band*: This one is on Vimeo rather than YouTube. Go to:
https://vimeo.com/124143248;
and then click the arrow button to run the video.

TUBA SKINNY'S CD - 'OWL CALL BLUES'

Tuba Skinny's CD *Owl Call Blues* was released at the end of August 2014.

I hope you will listen to it (on Bandcamp) and buy it if you haven't already done so.

The band's frequent guitarist Max Bien-Khan recorded the music with his equipment over several days in one of the New Orleans houses in which Tuba Skinny musicians live. The resulting acoustic is of a very high quality.

Here are some notes on what the CD contains:

1. Crazy 'Bout You: a standard Tuba Skinny performance of the pleasant, simple 16-bar tune, with singing by Erika and good ensemble work. I enjoyed Shaye's cheeky Ab on the very last note played - turning the final chord into Bb7th!

2. Rosa Lee Blues: vocal by Greg (abetted by Erika) in this 12-bar blues, which is slightly unusual in having an eight-to-the-bar rhythm and being played in the key of G.

3. Cannonball Blues: An amazing key-changing 12-bar blues with a terrific head arrangement. I love the moment when Shaye shakes her cornet though about 12 notes in half a second while changing the key from Eb to Ab! And it's clever how they slide down to the Key of C for Todd's tuba chorus before sliding up again to Ab.

4. Got a Mind To Ramble: One of those Erika vocals that we all love. Essentially a simple 8-bar theme in Bb - just the sort of material out of which nobody can make more than Erika and Tuba Skinny do.

5. Short-Dress Gal: Many of us know and love the 1927 original by the Sam Morgan Band. Tuba Skinny recreate it with their usual skill and Barnabus does a great job on the trombone, in the style of Big Jim Robinson on the Sam Morgan recording.

6. Owl Call Blues: I think for many of us this haunting song alone is worth the price of the CD. Shaye and Erika composed it; and here the band performs it lyrically for us.

7. Too Tight: The bouncy 16-bar blues highlights the strings and also Todd on the tuba.

8. Oriental Strut: Johnny St. Cyr's complex multi-part 1926 composition is very well executed, with a typical Tuba Skinny arrangement including some tricky breaks and rhythmic effects.

9. Ambulance Man: This 1930 Hattie Hart song is a duet with a story to tell. There is very good ensemble support. Basically a 12-bar Chorus in Bb but with a preceding Verse.

10. How Do They Do It That Way?: This Victoria Spivey song from 1929 is a favourite with the band and their followers. There are plenty of videos of them performing it. And it's a number they have recorded twice for CDs: it was also on their *Garbage Man* CD. So we are in familiar territory, though with a new arrangement. On this occasion they have chosen to play one Chorus in Eb and then one in Bb (Erika's preferred key) before Erika's vocal solo. But they return to Eb for a remarkable final Chorus, displaying Shaye's talents as she plays almost the entire Chorus solo, against stop chords.

11. Dallas Rag: This tune (devised and recorded by The Dallas String Band in 1927) has settled into Tuba Skinny's repertoire. Although it's based on a simple chord sequence, given its liveliness and the use of breaks, it is a great fun number. Good work all round. Fans of Robin will enjoy hearing him strut his stuff.

12. Untrue Blues: Another 8-bar theme bouncily played and well sung by Erika. You'll enjoy hearing Shaye playing the fiddle here. Like Rosa Lee Blues (above) it's played in G.

13. Somebody's Been Lovin' My Baby: One of those sad tales that suits Erika's voice very well. A 32-bar song. It sounds like another example of a key that is hardly ever ventured into by other traditional jazz bands - A minor.

14. Willie the Weeper: Jazz bands have been playing this one since 1920. The musicians of Tuba Skinny give a lusty creative performance, almost entirely with full ensemble and preferring the keys of G minor and Bb to those used by many bands - D minor and F. (By the way, Robin told me this is his favourite track on the CD).

15. Travellin' Blues: A standard 12-bar, with Shaye on fiddle and Greg providing the vocal - again abetted by Erika.

TUBA SKINNY'S CD - 'BLUE CHIME STOMP'

We are told this CD was recorded at The Tigermen Den in Royal Street, New Orleans. The building is situated in a peaceful spot about three-quarters of a mile east of the French Quarter. It is a restored 1830s corner store. It seems there is plenty of music and dancing there these days, and that great food is served.

Maybe the aim was to get an appropriate 'old-time dance hall' type of acoustic. (You may remember The Shotgun Jazz Band did just that by recording a CD in the former Luthjen's Dance Hall.)

There is certainly a good sound quality to this CD. As soon as it begins, with a lusty performance of *Maple Leaf Rag*, you realise you can hear the tones of all the individual instruments very clearly. Turn up the volume and it's like having them in the room with you.

You later find that, in the recording process, Erika's voice has fared just a little less well in a couple of numbers than the instruments. She is a wonderful singer in great form and beloved by us all but listen to her performance of her own composition *Broken-Hearted Blues* on the band's 2009 CD and then listen to her performance of the same song on this 2016 CD. A big difference, isn't there? In the 2009 version, the voice is completely clear and you can make out all the words easily; but you can't *quite* say the same about the 2016 version.

The band has evolved, of course. In 2009, they had just five musicians, plus Erika singing. But in the 2016 CD, they sometimes use nine musicians (three of them reed men) in addition to Erika. This has made Tuba Skinny sound more like a 'big band' on a few numbers. Especially when they use a driving saxophone and 'walking' riffs (as in *Running Down My Man* and *Broken-Hearted Blues*) we seem to be in the realms of R&B music. Indeed a correspondent told me the Tuba Skinny website - introducing this CD - said '*...this album features us in a couple different line-ups - our traditional one, as well as one with multiple reed players, and also our R&B line-up including piano, upright bass and drum set*'.

There is also inevitably a greater sense of choreography these days. In the more complicated multi-theme tunes, such as *Soudan*, *Oh Papa*, Shaye's composition *Blue Chime Stomp*, the vigorous *Variety Stomp* and - to a lesser extent - *Dear Almanzoer*, all the musicians had to master their parts meticulously in order to participate in the strict, tight arrangements. Of course there is still some room for free expression and improvising, but the backbone of each of these pieces is rigid.

Robin Rapuzzi plays the full drum-kit on some of these numbers. Todd Burdick apparently plays the string bass rather than the tuba on some - but I have yet to work out which, though I think they include *Running Down My Man*. He told me in 2016 that he had been 'learning to play a string bass' but he did not mention that he had already recorded with it!

The barrel-house piano (presumably the one belonging to The Tigermen Den) is played by Shaye on some of the pieces. One of these - *I'm Blue and Lonesome* - is heard in the key of Gb. Amazing. When did you last hear a tune performed by a jazz band in Gb? I can't recall when. All other bands would simply have opted for a key of G or F to keep the playing simpler.

And on the same subject, Erika sings *Running Down My Man* (the Merline Johnson 12-bar from 1936) in E - a key most traditional jazz musicians steer clear of.

These two tunes make me suspect the piano was half a tone flat. After all, in YouTube videos (with Shaye on cornet rather than piano) they have always played *Running Down My Man* in F and *I'm Blue and Lonesome* in G. But for the CD Shaye switched to the piano. If, as I believe, it was half a tone flat, then its F actually produced an E and its G sounded like Gb. Perhaps that's the complete explanation. The rest of the band did very well to adapt to such awkward keys.

With very neat banjo support, Erika sings *Me and My Chauffeur* (the song written by E. Lawler and recorded in 1941 by Memphis Minnie). This is trickier to sing than it may sound: note the long pause that has to be left in the ninth and tenth bars. There are some gems from Erika - not only those I have mentioned but also the 12-bar blues (composed in the 1930s by Ann Turner for Georgia White) *Almost Afraid To Love*, and *Oh Papa* (the Ma Rainey number from 1927) and *Midnight Blues*, both with substantial vocals.

Anyone who has watched the YouTube videos of Tuba Skinny to emerge since March 2015 will have heard all of the tunes on this CD, so they may already be familiar to you.

But here are a few more thoughts about some of the pieces.

Soudan started out in about 1906 as a sort of tone poem for piano by the Czech composer Gabriel Sebek. He called it *Oriental Scene for Piano, Opus 45*. The sub-title was *In The Soudan: A Dervish Chorus*. The ODJB recorded an adaptation of it in 1917 as *Oriental Jazz* (or *Jass*) and recorded it again in 1920 - this time as *Soudan*. As I have indicated, Tuba Skinny play a neat, strict arrangement. Their version intersperses the 'oriental' theme in F minor with the more bouncy traditional theme in the related key of Ab, and there is a trombone-led F minor coda from Barnabus to round it off. It's a very unusual number!

Corrine (sung by Erika) is *not* the same as the famous *Corrine Corrina. Corrine,* recorded in 1937 by Blind Boy Fuller, is a 16-bar blues, not a 12-bar. Erika gives a fine performance in the key of A, appropriately supported by the resonator guitar.

Memphis Shake (long-since established in Tuba Skinny's repertoire) is a straightforward number of two short themes and distinctive diminished chords. The 'big band' line-up gives it a delightfully free treatment, with much ensemble work.

Similar is *Shake It And Break It* (which has two short themes - in minor and major keys). The performance is very enjoyable and the final minutes are taken up with some pretty soloing and ensemble on the major-key theme.

Blue Chime Stomp is of course yet another fine composition by Shaye.

The CD ends with a very pleasant and straightforward version of *Chloe* - bringing things full circle in a sense, as this number also featured sweetly on their very first CD of seven years earlier, when they had only five musicians: a cornet, violin and trombone were supported merely by a tuba and guitar. This latest CD version of *Chloe* (using at least eight musicians) is taken a shade more slowly.

I must also mention the order in which the tunes have been thoughtfully arranged on the CD: fast and slow numbers alternate, as do instrumentals and vocals. So, played straight through, it makes a good concert.

Our heroine - the multi-talented Shaye – did the artwork for the CD.

TUBA SKINNY'S CD - 'TUPELO PINE'

Tuba Skinny recorded their eighth album - *Tupelo Pine* - in May 2017 and released it in August that year.

Using the eight musicians who were appearing regularly with the band at the time (but without Erika, who was absent), it offers music ranging from 1921 right up to tunes recently composed by three of the band members. Greg provides vocals, with one by Max.

The only tune to have appeared previously on one of their CDs is *Call of the Freaks*. On their earlier *Garbage Man* CD, it was played under its alternative title, which is in fact *Garbage Man*. In this 2017 version, there are some 'freakish' inventions, especially from the clarinet, and we still have the vocal (*Take out your can....*). But the arrangement is more elaborate, intricate, delicate, and polished than in the earlier version.

And that is exactly what will strike you about this album. Everything is so deftly executed. You have the impression that a great deal of preparation has gone into the arrangements. Backing rhythmic patterns are precise and well-rehearsed. All the little breaks are carefully worked out. A good illustration of this is the structure and use of two-bar breaks in *Come On and Stomp, Stomp, Stomp*, where the band precisely follows the famous recording made in 1927 by Johnny Dodds' Black Bottom Stompers. What stands out strongly compared with Tuba Skinny's earlier recordings is that everything is even more slick and polished.

As usual with Tuba Skinny, there is no exhibitionism. The emphasis is on good melodic music played with bags of intelligence and impeccable teamwork.

Several of the tunes are familiar to anyone who watched YouTube videos in 2016 and 2017. For example, the 1933 Clarence Williams composition *Chocolate Avenue* is yet another of those good old numbers the band unearthed. It is a gently swinging 32-bar tune in Eb; and the band passes the melody around in its usual fashion. You will notice the trombonist Barnabus Jones leading the first sixteen bars of the Second Chorus and Craig on clarinet leading from the Middle Eight to the end of the Chorus. In the third Chorus Todd on sousaphone is given the dominant role in the first sixteen bars but the full ensemble rounds the piece off. So: three Choruses in all.

And Clifford Hayes' romping *Frog Hop* from 1929 (at two and a half minutes the shortest piece in the album) is a real foot-tapper, with good little solos and a couple of amusing 'frog' effects.

Dangerous Blues - the 1921 song with music by that tragically short-lived young lady Billie Browne - features Craig on clarinet and also has the usual collective vocal.

Come On and Stomp, Stomp, Stomp (composed in 1927 by Fats Waller *et al.*) is the trickiest and most complex piece in this album. Tuba Skinny's version is taken at a more leisurely pace than the one by Johnny Dodds, is fully arranged, complete with the key changes, and sets a great example to any band wishing to try this tune.

Shaye's composition *Pearl River Stomp* (2016) is a bouncy 16-bar number and in this performance the lead is passed around, the bass clarinet is strongly in evidence and there is even a 'twos' section shared by cornet and trombone.

And Shaye's *Nigel's Dream* (from 2015) is another fine

composition. With typical Shaye-isms, it slides neatly from C to Eb, back to C and then back to Eb to finish. It uses a thematic base reminiscent of the middle eight of *East Coast Trot*, and indeed the whole piece is something of a trot, played with great energy. Quite a dream our Nigel had!

I am glad the album also includes *Thoughts*, Robin Rapuzzi's gently rolling composition from 2015, in a lovely arrangement.

I'm Going to Germany (the 1929 number composed by Noah Lewis for Cannon's Jug Stompers) is a 16-bar song with a wistful melody, well presented by Greg, with good support from the band.

Greg also sings *Loose Like That* - one of those bright 8-bar tunes from which Tuba Skinny always manages to extract so much. It gets the album off to a fine start. (There is a YouTube video of them playing this song at the Abita Springs Buskers' Festival in April 2017.) In contrast, he also sings the 1930 Broonzy number *Eagle Riding Papa*, which is a brisk 32-bar tune.

Max is the singer on *Right or Wrong*, the pleasant love song composed in 1921 by Arthur Sizemore and Paul Biese, with words by Haven Gillespie.

Many fans have said that the elegiac minor-key *Deep Bayou Moan* is the loveliest melody Shaye has ever written. She herself leads it off, and it is then played beautifully by all members of the band. You may well consider this track alone justifies the price of the album.

The eponymous *Tupelo Pine*, composed by Barnabus Jones (possibly as a tribute to his famous dog!) is a slow, lovely melody in Eb over a simple chord progression (plenty of Ebs,

C7ths and Abs). As with all the other tunes, it provides opportunities for a variety of instruments to take the lead.

MAKING MUCH OUT OF SIMPLE MATERIAL

Tuba Skinny are fond of what I would describe as 'eight-bar melodies'. What I am referring to are themes of eight bars (measures), sometimes repeated, so you could say the tunes are either of eight bars or sixteen bars (often with a 'turn-around' in bars 7 and 8). A sixteen bar (8 + 8) example is *Late Hour Blues* - a song they introduced into their repertoire in April 2015.

I suppose this is inevitable with a band that garners so much of its material from the unsophisticated songs of the jug bands and blues guitarists of the 1920s and 1930s. They went in for simple, memorable themes that are really good to sing.

These eight-bar tunes (sometimes using only two chords and sometimes needing just four chords covering two bars each) have become specialities of Tuba Skinny's wonderful vocalist, Erika Lewis.

Not long ago, she added *Untrue Blues* to her eight-bar songs in a version that is remarkably faithful to the 1937 original by Blind Boy Fuller. Incidentally, Tuba Skinny play it in the key of A, which is awkward for some brass and clarinet players. For Erika singing it, type 'Tuba Skinny -Untrue Blues - FQF 4/13/14' into YouTube. In the original, Blind Boy Fuller preferred the key of Bb.

But other Tuba Skinny numbers in this eight-bar category are:
Mississippi River Blues (Big Bill Broonzy, 1934)
Blue Spirit Blues (by Spencer Williams and famously recorded by Bessie Smith in 1929; it also has a 12-bar theme at the end)
Got a Mind To Ramble (Merline Johnson, 1930s)

Lonesome Drag (Tennessee Chocolate Drops, 1930; adapted by Erika Lewis)
Ice Man (Memphis Minnie, 1936)
Baby, Please Don't Go ('Big Joe' Williams, 1935)
I'll See You in the Spring (The Memphis Jug Band, 1927)
Owl Call Blues (music by Shaye Cohn and words by Erika Lewis, 2014)
Papa, Let Me Lay It On You (Blind Boy Fuller, 1938)
Too Tight Blues (Blind Blake, 1927)
All I Want is a Spoonful (Papa Charlie Jackson, 1925)

There's a lesson here for the rest of us. Maybe we should play more eight-bar tunes, especially if our band is lucky enough to have a singer.

A VISIT TO BACCHANAL

BACCHANAL doesn't look much from the outside. But it has become in recent years a very important jazz venue.

Where is it? At 600 Poland Avenue, New Orleans. This is in the Bywater district of the City. The building is situated close to the Mississippi, about 1¾ miles east of the French Quarter. So it is some distance from the famous jazz venues and clubs of Frenchmen Street.

Essentially it is a very well stocked wine shop. But behind the shop there is an extensive back yard. It is open seven days a week from 11a.m. until midnight and excellent meals are available.

Jazz bands are regularly booked and at the far end of the courtyard there is a stage on which they perform.

How did I get to know about this? Robin Rapuzzi e-mailed to tell me Tuba Skinny would be playing there on the evening of February 14, 2017, a few hours after my wife and I were due to land at New Orleans Airport. He thought we would like the venue if we could make it in time. *We* thought it would be a good way to celebrate our 57th wedding anniversary.

We caught the second set and I tried to video the band. It was not easy because the courtyard was crowded with noisy, happy people. However, I hope the results (Tuba Skinny playing two tunes - (1) a new composition by the band's Tomas Majcherski (it is called 'The Tag Along Blues') and (2) Piron's 'Bouncing Around') will give you some idea of the atmosphere at Bacchanal; and perhaps you may be interested in visiting the place for yourself one of these days. Watch the videos by going to YouTube and typing in 'Tuba Skinny: The Tag Along Blues' and 'Tuba Skinny: Bouncing Around'.

A few moments later, the skies opened and rain fell heavily. The band and some of the audience adjourned via the outside staircase to the attic that is visible at the very end of the 'Bouncing Around' video. The band squeezed into a corner and played a few more tunes but conditions for making videos were unfavourable.

'ALLIGATOR CRAWL'

In the beginning there was a composition by the young Fats Waller. He probably composed it in 1927 and he called it *Alligator Crawl*. It acquired words by Andy Razaf, so it was also available as a song: *Alligator Crawl is so appealing - A creepy rhythm that will tickle your toes. Never fails to bring a happy feeling - Its tempo has a charm that grows and grows* .... etc.

In 1934, Fats Waller himself recorded it as a piano solo. His version makes it sound like a boogie-woogie blended with a rocking catchy song. I believe this version is still popular as a party piece for solo pianists. Bert Brandsma has kindly supplied me with an analysis of the structure:

1. 16 bars in C (2 times 8)
2. The 24 bar A B A form in C
Modulation to F
3. Theme in F

But in May 1927, Louis Armstrong and his Hot Seven (including Johnny Dodds on clarinet, Johnny St. Cyr on guitar and Pete Briggs on tuba) had made a lusty three-minute recording in Chicago of *Alligator Crawl*. Their version has not much in common with the later recording by Fats Waller. Instead of the 16-bar sections (8 + 8 bars) it has four 12-bar blues sequences. It plays the 24-bar theme only once (from 1 min. 10 secs. to 2 mins. 05 secs. during the performance). Although these 24 bars seem (to my ear) to use the same harmonic sequence as Fats Waller, Louis plays a melody that is almost totally different, apart from the famous opening two bars. So, in effect, only 55 seconds of Armstrong's 3-minute recording sound anything like Waller's. In most respects the Hot Seven interpretation is so different from the other that the two versions sound like two different pieces of music.

This led me to speculate that Armstrong (and his pianist wife Lil Hardin) took just a musical idea and the harmonies from the Waller 24-bar theme and re-structured them in their own way, allowing for some tremendous fresh invention. My guess was that Lil Hardin's was the brain behind the project. With her classical training and skills as a jazz composer and arranger (constantly in use with this band in the mid-1920s), not to mention that she plays the piano on the recording, I would not be surprised if there is as much Hardin as Waller in the Hot Seven 1927 recording. Even the four 12-bar blues sequences (especially the ensemble one that is repeated) in the Armstrong version are not any old improvisations: they are majestic - and linger in our minds.

But the great Australian jazz researcher Bill Haesler has pointed out to me that there is also a richly-orchestrated and precisely-played recording of *Alligator Crawl* by 'Doc' Cook and His Doctors of Syncopation. This recording appears to have been made only a month after that of the Hot Seven. You can find it on YouTube and you will note that the composer is definitely given as Waller *and* that it includes some 12-bar sections reminiscent of Armstrong's, as well as the 24-bar theme.

Could the Hot Seven have started by looking at the same musical arrangement that Doc Cook used so precisely - re-interpreting it freely in their own way? Quite probably.

So I have to come to the conclusion that Waller probably wrote a 12-bar theme as well as the famous 24-theme when he originally composed the piece, but that he chose to re-write the tune, dropping the 12-bar theme and replacing it with some new 16-bar material, when he came to record it as a piano speciality seven years later.

Unless somebody finds a manuscript or orchestration from 1927, we may never know the full story.

Bill Haesler also pointed me to Ricky Ricardi's *Dippermouth Blogspot*, where Armstrong's performance is analysed and the writer also provides this information: *'Alligator Crawl' was originally titled 'House Party Stomp' and 'Charleston Stomp' before publisher Joe Davis gave it the final title.*

A theory of Erwin Elvers of Luetjensee, Germany, is that the *Alligator Crawl* played by Armstrong was based on a Spencer Williams composition from which Fats Waller adopted the 24-theme for his own composition. But this theory - though it appeals to me as plausible - seems unsupported by paper records. See Dick Baker's research at http://dickbaker.org/stompoff/index.pdf.

Parlophone put out a version with the title as *Alligator Blues* and the composer as 'Williams'. Perhaps that's what influenced Erwin Elvers; but both the title and the composer on this label are surely incorrect.

Adding a little to the confusion, some early Armstrong recordings do indeed give the tune the alternative title of *Alligator Blues*; and there actually is a tune called *Alligator Blues* that was recorded also in 1927 by a band called John Hyman's Bayou Stompers, but I can assure you Hyman's is a totally different piece of music. (John Hyman was the name used at the time by the cornet player John Wigginton Hyman - later better known as Johnny Wiggs). And adding still more confusion, there is a 1927 recording by Fess Williams' Royal Flush Orchestra of *Alligator Crawl*. It includes echoes of the 12-bar theme but not of the 24-bar, as far as I can tell.

Whoever was responsible for 'composing' its melodies and arranging its structure, it's the Hot Seven version that most bands try to copy these days. Fortunately the Hot Seven recording has survived the passage of time really well. It's there for us all to study. Its structure is as follows. It comprises eight segments:

1. Introduction : 2 bars (cornet) in the key of F.
2. 12-bar Blues in F, solo clarinet.
3. 12-bar Blues in F, ensemble.
4. 4-bar Modulation, clever, mainly on G7, leading to a change to the key of C.
5. 24-Bar Theme ensemble (structured a - b - a) in the key of C (the phrase given above appears in the 'a' parts; and the 'b' part uses some minor chords).
6. One bar in which Louis modulates the key back to F (making the previous theme virtually stretch to a highly unusual 25 bars).
7. 12-Bar blues in F, guitar.
8. As No. 3 above: 12-bar blues in F, ensemble, with athletic improvisations by Louis.

And if you would like to examine the 21st-Century version by Tuba Skinny, I can tell you they recorded it on their *Pyramid Strut* CD, and you can watch them (on YouTube, thanks to the generosity of the great video-maker *digitalalexa*) playing it in public. You will find that Tuba Skinny take the tune a shade more slowly than Louis but they follow meticulously the structure and spirit of his recording, right down to that 'extra' bar I have called Segment 6 (watch out for it at precisely 2 mins. 13 secs. into the video). But of course, being Tuba Skinny, they (in particular Shaye on cornet) have introduced exciting alternative improvised phrasings of their own. Watch the performance on YouTube by typing in 'Tuba

Skinny - Alligator Crawl - Terra Blues 8/19/14' (it's https://www.youtube.com/watch?v=ZRLfaJBUlls).

'ALL I WANT IS A SPOONFUL'

One of the delightful videos of Tuba Skinny put up on YouTube by the generous and indefatigable film-makers codenamed *digitalalexa* (Al and his wife Judy) - to whom we should all be deeply grateful - is a song called *All I Want is a Spoonful*, played in Bb. It is essentially a simple eight-bar theme.

Erika plays the drum and sings the words, accompanied by five members of the band and their dog - and another dog who seems keen to make friends with Robin. Shaye plays both the fiddle and the cornet. And there is a fun chorus nicely played by Todd on the tuba, against stop-chords. You can get to this video by typing in 'Tuba Skinny- At The Mill- All I Want'.
(The video is https://www.youtube.com/watch?v=D8RVajzeDQM)

It was a new song to me, though I found it was recorded in 1925 by 'Papa' Charlie Jackson, who probably also wrote it.

It's a tune firmly demonstrating the popular chord progression known as *The Salty Dog Chord Sequence*.

Tunes with this sequence begin (usually two bars) on the chord of the 6th note in the scale (e.g., a tune in the key of Bb starts on the chord of G or G7th). This is normally followed by the chord on the 2nd note of the scale, and then on the 5th note of the scale, thus continuing the 'circle of fifths'.

Examples of tunes following *The Salty Dog Chord Sequence* are:

A Good Man Is Hard To Find
Alabamy Bound

All I Want Is A Spoonful
Any Time
At The Jazz Band Ball [main strain]
Balling The Jack
Friends and Neighbours
Good Time Flat Blues (also known as *Farewell to Storyville*) [chorus]
Jazz Me Blues [main strain]
Louis-i-a-ni-a
Put and Take Blues
Rose of the Rio Grande
Salty Dog [the archetype]
Seems Like Old Times
Shine On Harvest Moon
Sweet Georgia Brown
Tailgate Ramble
There'll Be Some Changes Made
Up A Lazy River
You've Got The Right Key But The Wrong Keyhole

'ALMOST AFRAID TO LOVE'

Tuba Skinny has given us a mind-boggling performance that serves as a lesson to us all. We again have to thank the generous and prolific film-maker *digitalalexa* for uploading it to YouTube. (I will give you the link to it shortly.)

I am speaking about *Almost Afraid to Love*. This is a song I had never heard of. But banjo-player Stan Cummings of Sacramento kindly informed me it was composed by Ann Turner in 1938 and made famous at that time by the great blues singer Georgia White.

On the face of it, no performance could be simpler. It's just seven choruses of a 12-bar blues in C - 84 bars of music in all.

But the way it is interpreted is exemplary - demonstrating all that is great about traditional jazz at its best. Just listen.

Chorus 1: Against a solid foundation provided by the tuba, washboard, guitar and bass drum, the cornet introduces us to the tune; but the music is like a conversation between three old friends. Using her cup mute, Shaye makes the sad statements and Barnabus (trombone) and Ewan (clarinet) respond sympathetically to everything the cornet says.

Chorus 2: Erika begins to sing, telling the story with an uncluttered accompaniment. What a solid foundation Todd gives (as usual) on the tuba!

Chorus 3: Erika completes the story - with Shaye providing tasteful background colouring, using the cup mute.

Chorus 4: Ensemble. Both the cornet and trombone are muted now. This is another chorus sounding like a conversation between three old friends. It reminds me of the string quartets of Haydn and Mozart. Some of the phrases are exquisite - such as Shaye's phrase responding to the trombone at 1 min. 49secs. [I think this must be one of Shaye's favourite phrases - you hear it frequently in her playing.]

Chorus 5: The 'conversation' continues; with Evan making assertive statements on his clarinet, while the cornet and trombone reply 'Yes, we know. It's a shame. You're so right!'

Chorus 6: Erika resumes the song.

Chorus 7: Erika completes the song, but with the others performing like the Greek Chorus from *Oedipus Rex* - commenting sympathetically on the events of the story. It is outstandingly good four-part interplay with the singer. And as the performance comes to an end, there's one more surprise in store. Shaye picks up her 'jam funnel' mute for a strong conclusive effect in the final two bars, descending a C minor arpeggio.

There is nothing strenuous or over-loud or showy or strident about this performance. There are no screaming high notes. The playing gives the illusion of being totally relaxed, simple and effortless. But the apparent simplicity conceals art of the highest order.

To watch it, type in 'Tuba Skinny - Almost Afraid to Love - Royal St. 4/8/13'.

'BEER GARDEN BLUES'

Be honest. Had you ever heard of *Beer Garden Blues* before Tuba Skinny unearthed it and started performing it in 2015? I certainly had not.

Robin Rapuzzi told me it is a tune the band now particularly enjoys.

The music was written in 1933 by Lewis Raymond and Clarence Williams; and lyrics were contributed by Walter Bishop.

It is normally played in the key of F, but making great use of the related key of D minor. In fact, a distinctive characteristic of the song is its strong minor flavour - in both Verse and Chorus.

The Verse comprises 16 bars. The Chorus has a 32-bar A-A-B-A structure.

You can hear the original Clarence Williams version on YouTube by typing in 'Clarence Williams - Beer Garden Blues'. Surprisingly, the band omits the Verse but works its way through the Chorus five times (thus playing 5×32 = 160 bars in total). Much use is made of breaks, especially on Bars 23 and 24 of every Chorus; and the third Chorus is led by the washboard, with the others providing punctuation.

Clearly, Williams treated his own music very freely when he came to perform it. And Tuba Skinny do the same, making great use of the rhythms and the harmonies, but with slightly less than scrupulous respect for the original melody. For a performance by them, type in
'Beer Garden Blues - Tuba Skinny'. This should bring you to a video filmed by my friend James Sterling

(https://www.youtube.com/watch?v=fm239UIkaQ4). They play through the Chorus six times [no Verse] on lines very similar to those of the Williams recording.

'BELLAMINA'

In the 1920s, there was a white ship named *Bellamina*, based at Nassau in the Bahamas. It was used for smuggling spirits 200 miles across the sea to Florida. But the American Coast Guards intercepted it.

After the boat's release, it was taken to dry dock in Nassau - this time to be painted BLACK!

The Bahamians loved inventing songs about anything in the news; and so a great 16-bar simple rhythmic song soon appeared.

Bellamina, Bellamina!
Bellamina's in the harbour.
Bellamina, Bellamina!
Bellamina's in the harbour.
So put the Bellamina on the dock
And paint the Bellamina black, black!
Oh put the Bellamina on the dock
And paint the Bellamina black!

In fact, there were at least three more ships that had to be repainted in this way. They are all mentioned in the version of the song that you can listen to by going to YouTube and typing in 'Blind Blake - A Second Album of Bahamian Songs (1952)'. At 2 minutes 47 seconds, Blind Blake (who was recording this in 1952) sings several verses, mentioning other ships; and you can pick out the words very clearly.

That great benefactor of all jazz musicians - Lasse Collin - has provided us with the music. See:
http://cjam.lassecollin.se/

Put simply, the chord sequence is:

I	I	I	V7
V7	V7	V7	I
I	IV	V7	I
I	IV	V7	I

Lasse was doubtless inspired to do this by Tuba Skinny, who in 2017 revived this fine old song, with Greg Sherman singing the vocal and the whole band showing what great jazz musicians can do with a simple theme: their performance of *Bellamina* lasts five and a half minutes.

As you can see, Lasse has put it in the key of Eb (as played by Tuba Skinny) and he has provided a lead-sheet in F for the benefit of Bb instrument players.

James Sterling kindly videoed the Tuba Skinny performance for us. To view it in YouTube, type in 'Bellamina - Tuba Skinny'. James has pointed out to me that there is also a recording of this song by *The Nassau String Band* made on a field trip by John Lomax as long ago as 1935: Type in 'Nassau String Band - Bellamina (Bahamas, 1935)'.

There! With so much to help us, those of us who are musicians have no excuse for leaving this number out of our repertoire. It's a good one to play. It's catchy, easy to improvise on; and it offers some rhythmic variety to our programme.

This is one of the many excellent 16-bar tunes available to traditional jazz bands. We should always have two or three of them in our programmes. Others include *Up Jumped the*

Devil, *Winin' Boy Blues*, *Satan Your Kingdom Must Come Down* and *Rip 'Em Up Joe*.

Let's hear more bands playing *Bellamina*!

'BLUE CHIME STOMP'

Tuba Skinny (and more specifically Shaye Cohn) did it again: in early-2015 they came up with a new tune and gave it a brilliant performance from which we can all learn something.

I am referring to *Blue Chime Stomp* which - thanks to the prolific video-maker codenamed *RaoulDuke504* - became the newest tune in their YouTube repertoire on 24 March 2015. Have a listen by typing into YouTube 'Tuba Skinny - Blue Chime Stomp'. This should take you to https://www.youtube.com/watch?v=Cb1134T4BUM.

Great stuff, isn't it?

Underlying all the excitement and brilliance, the tune comprises just two 16-bar themes, both played in the key of Bb. Let's call them A and B.

The A Theme includes the 'Chimes' - descending in semitones over bars 1 - 4 and 9 - 12.

The B Theme is sprightly and melodious. Using a comfortable chord progression (you find something very similar in *Do What Ory Say* and *Dallas Rag* and *Sister Kate* and *South*), it lends itself easily to improvisations.

The band plays the themes in this order:
A-A-B-B-A-B-B-B-A-B-B

As usual, Tuba Skinny add sparkle, brilliance and excitement to the basic material. This includes playing the 'chimes' in different ways - such as hitting the second beat of the bar rather than the first, and breaking each chime into four single notes played by the tuba, trombone, cornet and clarinet successively over the four beats of a bar.

And when they play Theme B, they build up the excitement like this:
5th time: Clarinet alone leads;
6th time: Clarinet gets support from the trombone;
7th time : Cornet joins in, for a thrilling energetic polyphonic chorus.

There are no tedious 'solo' choruses. Except as mentioned above, the full ensemble keeps busy throughout.

ERIKA'S 'BROKEN-HEARTED BLUES'

One of the loveliest uses of the Magnolia Chord Progression is to be heard in *Broken-Hearted Blues*, the 2009 composition written and sung by Erika Lewis with Tuba Skinny. This song is played in the key of C and the Magnolia Progression occurs several times. You can hear Erika perform the song on their 2009 CD or by watching a video uploaded by James Sterling: go to YouTube and type in 'Tuba Skinny - Erika's Broken Hearted Blues'.

By the way, the other *Broken-Hearted Blues* - the quite different song composed in 1937 by Lil Johnson - is also played by Tuba Skinny and there are several videos of that song. Don't be confused.

The Magnolia Chord Progression is one with which several of the good old songs begin: start on the tonic chord; then the tonic 7th; then the chord of the 4th note in the scale; and then the 4th minor (or sometimes diminished).

So, in the Key of C, this means:
 C : C7 : F : Fm
It's known to jazzmen as *The Magnolia Progression* because it was used to begin the chorus of the famous 1928 Jimmy McHugh and Dorothy Fields jazz tune *Magnolia's Wedding Day*.
As you can see from the chords, it makes for a bright, positive start in the home key but gets you into a minor - with possibly just a hint of sadness - by the fourth bar.

This effect is particularly noticeable in the opening chords of *Cherry Red* and *Mississippi River Blues* (which Tuba Skinny sometimes perform as *Big Boat*). These are both 8-bar blues. It also appears at the start of *Girl of My Dreams*, *Got a Mind* to Ramble, In the Upper Garden, My Mother's Eyes, Old Rocking Chair, When You and I Were Young, Maggie, When the Swallows Come Back to Capistrano, I'll See You in the Spring, Does Jesus Care?, Lonesome Road, Louisiana Fairytale, I May Be Wrong But I Think You're Wonderful, You Were Only Passing Time With Me, If I Had You, After My Laughter Came Tears, and *Carolina Moon*.

The Magnolia Progression is also used in some tunes where the 'saddening' effect is less obvious, though this is because they are generally brighter and faster. Examples are *'Deed I Do, Cornet Chop Suey, I'm Gonna Meet My Sweetie Now, I Want a Little Girl to Call My Own, I'm Putting All My Eggs in One Basket, Brown Skin Mamma,* the final theme of *Stevedore Stomp*, not to mention *Magnolia's Wedding Day* itself.

'CHOCOLATE AVENUE'

'Chocolate Avenue' is yet another obscure old tune tracked down by Tuba Skinny. We have to thank the band for reviving it after 90 years and for giving us such a delightful interpretation. We must also thank - as so often - the great video-maker *RaoulDuke504* for being there to film it for us and for identifying it when they introduced it.

It is one of the forgotten numbers by the prolific Clarence Williams.

Chocolate Avenue is a conventionally-structured 32-bar tune [A - A - B - A] in Eb. The only harmonic surprise is the second half of the fourth bar in the A sections, where the harmony appears to be Eb minor where the ear would expect Eb major.

I made a video of them playing this tune when I was in New Orleans in February 2017. It is at https://www.youtube.com/watch?v=Jnm7QBsnstg on YouTube. If you type in 'Tuba Skinny Chocolate Avenue', you should find various videos of it easily enough.

The band plays the tune gently, four times through, without any Introduction; and the melody lead is passed around among the instruments, as in most Tuba Skinny performances.

Note also that the band recorded this tune on their 2018 CD 'Tupelo Pine', so that's the best place to hear a good clear version.

'CRAZY BLUES'

My friend Jan, who lives in Holland, is a keen gardener and also a fan of Tuba Skinny. He is particularly fond of Erika's wonderful singing. He likes to work in his garden, with recordings of Erika to entertain him.

Jan told me how much he likes *Crazy Blues* - a 2014 addition to Tuba Skinny's repertoire. He admires the way Erika sings almost continuously through the entire 4½-minute performance. He says he considers it a 'masterpiece' because of the beauty of the song, the way Erika conveys the emotions and the perfect cooperation of the band in supporting Erika - without any instrumental solos.

Crazy Blues was composed in 1920 by 27-year-old Perry Bradford, who at the time was the musical director of the great early blues singer Mamie Smith. She recorded it that year with her *Jazz Hounds*. It was a hugely successful recording and is now considered by jazz and blues scholars to have been an important milestone in the history of our music.

Tuba Skinny model their version very closely on Mamie Smith's. They use the same Introduction and structure. The only significant difference is that - after the long vocal - Tuba Skinny add an instrumental ensemble once through the Section I shall call (C). I suppose that, on the Mamie Smith 1920 version, limitations of available recording time prevented the band from doing anything other than rounding the tune off very quickly.

It is indeed a *tour de force* by Erika. I don't know how she memorises so many songs of this type and sings them so well, apparently with no loss of voice. And at the most emotional moments in this song, she has to hit high Ebs, which are probably at the top of her vocal range.

It's a curiously structured song, though typical of its time. You can think of it as having 40 bars of 'Verse' leading into a 16-bar 'Chorus' (I'm calling the Chorus C) - making 56 bars in all. But the performers break down the 'Verse' into two parts of 28 bars (let's call that A) and 12 bars (let's call that B) respectively. Tuba Skinny plays the song entirely in the key of Eb and the structure (Introduction plus three themes) seems to me to be:

(Intro) Band: 4 bars.
(A) Erika: 28-bar theme, starting at *I can't sleep at Night; I can't eat a bite....* and ending at *My love for that man will always be.*
(C) Erika: CHORUS 16 bars *Now I Got The Crazy Blues......*and ending with *I ain't had nothin' but bad news; now I got the Crazy Blues.* Note how the band again uses the *motif* from the Introduction at the end of this.
(B) Erika: 12-bar blues theme, starting at *Now I can read his letters but I sure can't read his mind.*, ending *now I see my poor love was blind.*
(B) Erika: 12-bar blues melody again, but with a different set of words, starting at *I went to the railroad.*
(C) Erika: CHORUS 16 bars *Now I Got The Crazy Blues.*
(C) Band: CHORUS 16 bars ensemble to round it off.

As so often, we must thank the great *digitalalexa* for filming this performance so brilliantly. Watch it by typing in YouTube 'Tuba Skinny Crazy Blues FQF 4/13/14'. As at the end of 2017, Erika had not recorded this song on any of the band's CDs.

Jan - the gentleman in Holland who first contacted me about this song - also kindly sent me the words:

Crazy Blues

I can't sleep at night.
I can't eat a bite
'Cause the man I love -
He don't treat me right.
He makes me feel so blue.
I don't know what to do.
Sometimes I sit and sigh
And then begin to cry
'Cause my best friend
Said his last goodbye.

There's a change in the ocean, change in the deep blue sea, my baby.
I'll tell you, folks, There ain't no change in me.
My love for that man will always be!

Now I got the crazy blues
Since my baby went away.
I ain't got no time to lose.
I must find him today.
Now the doctor's gonna
do all that he can,
But what you're gonna need
is an undertaker man.
I ain't had nothin' but bad news.
Now I got the crazy blues.

Now I can read his letters-
I sure can't read his mind.
I thought he's lovin' me.
He's leavin' all the time.
Now I see my poor love was blind.

I went to the railroad [to]
Hang my head on the track.

*Thought about my daddy-
I gladly snatched it back!
Now my babe's gone
And gave me the sack.*

*Now I've got the crazy blues
Since my baby went away.
I ain't had no time to lose.
I must find him today.*

*I'm gonna do like a Chinaman, go and get some hop -
Get myself a gun, and shoot myself a cop.
Ain't had nothin' but bad news
Now I've got the crazy blues.*

'CRAZY 'BOUT YOU'

'Crazy 'Bout You' is a great little 16-bar number that seems simple enough to play, with a straightforward chord progression.

It appears to have been written in about 1935 by blues harmonica player William 'Jazz Gillum' McKinley, who recorded it in Chicago that year with *The State Street Boys*.

You can hear his recording on YouTube by typing in 'Crazy 'Bout You – The State Street Boys (Big Bill Broonzy)'.

I first heard the tune in its more recent performances by Tuba Skinny, with a great vocal from Erika Lewis. On YouTube you can easily find the band performing the song at the Umbria Jazz Festival at the start of 2016. They have also recorded it and you can hear their spirited performance on their CD, *Owl Call Blues* (released in August 2014).

The lyrics? They seem to be on these lines:
Baby I'm crazy 'bout you.
Don't like the way you do.
Always mistreatin' me,
Say that you love me too.
Some day you'll want me
And I'll be far from you.
Then you will be sorry babe
You do me like you do.

A sad detail: poor William McKinley, the composer, was murdered at the age of 62, three years after he had retired from his career in music.

'DALLAS RAG'

On Tuba Skinny's 6th CD, *Owl Call Blues*, they included the tune *Dallas Rag*.

What a great tune! It's simple enough - a 4-bar introduction followed by two 16-bar themes both using a chord sequence that follows the *Sweet Sue Progression* and is rounded off with the *Sunshine Progression*. But it romps along when well played by a great band such as Tuba Skinny (who, by the way, must be credited with the recent revival of this fine old number).

There's also a great video uploaded by *digitalalexa* on YouTube of Tuba Skinny in March 2013 playing *Dallas Rag* in the French Quarter of New Orleans. They take it at a cracking pace and build in all kinds of variety in their treatment of the tune. You can watch it by typing in 'Tuba Skinny Dallas Rag Royal St. 4/13/13'. The musicians in the video include the great Jonathan Doyle and Ewan Bleach, whereas Craig Flory has replaced them on the latest CD.

Dallas Rag dates from 1927, when it was devised and recorded by *The Dallas String Band*. It could possibly have been composed by their Coley Jones, the mandolin player and leader of the group, but nobody knows for sure. If you wish, you can also find that original performance on YouTube.

'DANGEROUS BLUES'

There is so much joy in the history of traditional jazz. But frequently it is intermingled with sadness.

Here's a poignant example.

Dangerous Blues was recorded by The Original Dixieland Jazz Band in 1921. You can find the recording on YouTube. In more recent times, the tune has been revived by Tuba Skinny. They may be seen playing it in various YouTube videos and it is also on their 2017 CD 'Tupelo Pine'. It's a merry enough tune.

But here's the sad tale behind it. The composer of this song, Billie Brown, was a young lady who died of smallpox very soon after she composed it.

We know that is correct. But unfortunately not much else is known for sure about Billie.

Billie was probably born in 1903 and became something of a child prodigy. She first had some music published when she was only 12 years old. In the next few years, six more of her songs were published.

Billie's mother, Anna Welker Brown (who lived on until 1935), wrote lyrics to most of Billie's tunes, including the words for *Dangerous Blues*.

Billie's first song was published in Kansas City, and she is believed to have been living there with her mother in a rooming house at the time. One record suggests her mother may have been a music teacher (presumably she taught Billie) and that Billie worked as a pianist in a cafeteria. This was a time in history when it was still normal for children at such an age to have jobs rather than be in school.

By the time of *Dangerous Blues*, Billie had secured a job as a composer and pianist (piano and song demonstrator) for the J. W. Jenkins Music Company - a large and prosperous musical instrument dealer and music publisher. As well as *Dangerous Blues*, Jenkins published her *Lonesome Mama Blues* and *Lullaby Moon* - both very popular at the time - and also composed in 1921.

Dangerous Blues was a great success and Billie received a good deal of money from royalties during the weeks before she died. The blues singer Mamie Smith as well as The Original Dixieland Jazz Band immediately picked the tune up and recorded it.

And then - how awful! - poor young Billie contracted smallpox and by December 4th she was dead. What a terrible loss to the development of our music.

Another of Billie's songs - *What's On Your Mind?* - was published posthumously.

No sure evidence concerning Billie's father has been found, but he may have died earlier. Her mother Anna re-married when Billie was about 16 years old.

The crazy lyrics of *Dangerous Blues* appear to be:

Ta de da da de dum. Ta de da da de dum.
There's a funny strain a'stealing through my brain.
It drives me 'most insane it seems.
Ta de da da de dum. Ta de da da de dum.
If you listen now, I'll tell you what this
Ta da da de-dum means:

CHORUS:
Oh, I got them dangerous blues.
Naughty doggone dangerous blues.
Can't you hear the music playing soft and sweet?
It's the kind that makes you want to shake your feet.
I think I'm slippin'; I know I'm slippin'.
Ta de da de da de da de da de da de dum.
Weary, dreary dangerous blues;
they're the kind you hate to lose.
I can't even think,
So lay me out in pink.
Every time that saxophone it moans
I want to sink.
'Cause I got them doggone dangerous blues.
Oh, I got them dangerous blues.
Naughty doggone dangerous blues.
Can't you hear the music playing soft and sweet?
It's the kind that makes you want to shake your feet.
I think I'm slippin'; I know I'm slippin'.
Ta de da de da de da de da de da de dum.
Weary, dreary dangerous blues;
they're the kind you hate to lose.
I can't even think,
Can't even sleep a wink.
Every time I hear those mournful blues
I want to sink.
'Cause I got them doggone dangerous blues.

Footnote: a theory has been put forward that Billie was actually an adopted baby called Irene Anderson, who is believed to have been born in 1894 and adopted in 1895 by William Brown in Eureka Springs. This would have made her 27 when she died. But this theory raises troubling questions. How come Billie's age was given as 18 on her death certificate? How and why did it come about that her name changed from Irene to Billie? How is it that she and her mother are recorded as living in Kansas City, so far (250 miles) north of Eureka Springs? Why did the William Brown in question, still living in Eureka Springs in 1930, describe himself as a widower in the Census of that year?

I prefer to believe the details given on the Billie Brown's death certificate.

'DEAR ALMANZOER'

'Dear Almanzoer' was written and recorded in 1927 by Oscar Celestin. His version is on YouTube.

Listen to Celestin's version and then Tuba Skinny's. You will find the musicians of Tuba Skinny have kept faithfully to the original, even though their instrumentation is slightly different from Celestin's. The structure of Tuba Skinny's performance is as follows. The entire piece (which comprises three themes) is played in the key of Eb:

Theme A (played once): 16-bar theme like a Verse of a Song. Typical of verses in Eb, it ends on the chord of Bb7, leading perfectly into the tonic at the start of Theme B.

Theme B (played once): 32-bar theme (like a Chorus of a song).

Theme C: a 12-bar blues theme (played 5 times: i. clarinet against offbeats - exactly as on the Celestin version, ii. clarinet against stop chords - again exactly as on the Celestin version, iii. cornet, iv. trombone leading, v. trombone leading - with decoration from cornet).

Theme B: the 32-bar theme is played ensemble to finish (again as in the original Celestin performance).

I made a video of Tuba Skinny playing this tune. Type in 'Tuba Skinny play Dear Almanzoer' and this should bring you to https://www.youtube.com/watch?v=uIHM-V8pMiM.

This tune is also on their CD 'Blue Chime Stomp'.

'DEEP HENDERSON'

In 2013, Tuba Skinny added to their repertoire a piece written in 1926 by Fred Rose and first made famous that year by the King Oliver Band. It is called *Deep Henderson.*

They must have worked hard getting this tune into their heads. It is a tricky, complicated piece, including a key change (going from F into Db for the Trio, unlike the original piano sheet music). It has several sections and many moments where the clarinet or the cornet have one-bar breaks or where a beat or two are completely silent. It is also very rhythmic and the overall effect can be, I think, terrifically exciting. In the final theme (in Db), you can hear Shaye playing some astonishing, thrilling arpeggios.

Of all the Tuba Skinny tunes, this is probably the most complex.

You can hear them playing it on their CD 'Pyramid Strut'. There are also at least nine videos on YouTube of Tuba Skinny playing this tune. May I recommend that you seek them out?

'DELTA BOUND'

Delta Bound is a great haunting song: it descends through semitones, with a fair sprinkling of minor and diminished chords. It is a 32-bar tune, with the familiar a - a - b - a structure.

Those of us who are fans of Tuba Skinny (i.e. almost the entire population of the world) have been introduced to it through the singing of Erika Lewis. It was on Tuba Skinny's CD entitled *Rag Band* - released in 2012.

However, it seems the song dates from as long ago as 1934. It was composed by Alex Hill, who was a jazz pianist in Chicago during the 1920s. Although he worked with many of the 'big names', it is not surprising if you have never heard of Alex Hill. The poor chap lived only to the age of 30.

The band included this song on their CD 'Rag Band'. And on YouTube there is a video of Erika singing this song with Tuba Skinny in its early days. You can view it by typing in 'Tuba Skinny Delta Bound Live at the Hive 6-24-2011'. Erika sings *Delta Bound* in the key of Bb. However (typical of Tuba Skinny) the band usually plays a first chorus in the key of F before Erika takes over. The Band also reverts to F to round off the performance.

'DODO BLUES'

An unusual song in the Tuba Skinny repertoire is *Dodo Blues*. For a YouTube performance, type in 'Tuba Skinny Dodo Blues Rapperswil 30 juni 2013'.

However, for the existence of this song we must thank not some obscure hill-billy of the 1920s but rather the Australian blues singer and composer C. W. Stoneking. Born in Katherine, Australia, in 1974, this gentleman, of American parentage, became addicted to the raw blues as played in the 1920s and 1930s by such performers as Leroy Carr. Now, in the 21st Century, he writes, performs and sings in just that 1920s manner, together with his unusual backing group, *The Primitive Horn Orchestra* (who have more than a passing resemblance to Tuba Skinny).

C. W. Stoneking wrote *Dodo Blues* in about 2005 and you can also find him performing it on YouTube, where you will note that he performs it in the key of Ab, while Tuba Skinny prefer Eb, to suit Erika's voice.

If you want to add the tune to your repertoire or play along with it, you will find it easy to pick up. The main eight bars use the *Four-Leaf Clover Chord Progression*; and the Middle Eight chords are the same as those of dozens of other tunes (*Yes, Sir, That's My Baby*, *We'll Meet Again*, *On the Sunny Side of the Street*, for example).

My friend Tom Corcoran told me he saw C. W. Stoneking perform in Dublin. Tom said, 'He put on a fantastic show. His performance was a series of crazy stories interspersed with songs. and his banjo playing an absolute delight.'

'DO YOUR DUTY'

My ear was caught by the song *Do Your Duty*. It was written in 1933 by Wesley 'Sox' Wilson. He and his wife (Leola B. 'Coot' Grant) were vaudeville performers and song writers. It was recorded that year by the great Bessie Smith.

I am not sure whether Sox would agree with my attempt to transcribe his tune, but you can find my version on the internet at http://playing-traditional-jazz.blogspot.co.uk/2013/05/do-your-duty.html. It has a 32-bar structure, essentially four sets of 8 bars: a - a - b - a.

You can find this song on the Band's CD 'Six Feet Down'. Or, for a terrific street performance on YouTube, type in 'Tuba Skinny Do Your Duty Royal St 4/13/2012'.

'DUSTY RAG'

It was 23rd December 2015 and I started the day as usual by dealing with my large email jazz correspondence and then checking to see what was new on YouTube. I found that *RaoulDuke504* - the great Louisiana-based film-maker - had just put up another video of Tuba Skinny playing a few days earlier in the French Quarter.

On the faće of it, this video is nothing out of the ordinary. The tune is May Aufderheide's *Dusty Rag* (from 1908) in the sort of performance that the Tuba Skinny musicians probably regard as routine and unexceptional. They give a simple unpretentious interpretation, without special effects and complexities. What's more, there seems to have been a workman using an electric drill somewhere off-camera, so there are irritating occasional whirring noises in the background.

And yet, this is such an enjoyable performance that it reminds me why I consider the playing of Tuba Skinny to be streets ahead of most of the bands whose efforts I watch on YouTube.
The drumming (by Robin Rapuzzi) is so intelligent, tasteful and unobtrusive. The string players are completely solid in supplying accurate harmonies and four-to-the-bar rhythmic support. Todd Burdick (tuba - though he plays a sousaphone on this occasion) as ever provides a bass line that is elegant, accurate and appropriate. The 'front line' (clarinet, cornet and trombone) listen to each other carefully: they interweave their musical lines and harmonies with subtlety and with a total absence of flashiness or exhibitionism. The emphasis is on teamwork: players support each other. (Note how even when the sousaphone has a little 16-bar 'solo', Barnabus gives gentle support on the trombone.) Also, the band takes care with setting a perfect

tempo - and maintains it. Finally - and I think this is very important - there is no electronic amplification of any kind. Everyone plays acoustically. We can hear every instrument, and we can appreciate the various 'voices' and blending tones.

I hope you will share my pleasure. Type in 'Tuba Skinny – Dusty Rag'. If you are offered a choice of videos, click on the one uploaded by *RaoulDuke504.*

What makes other bands less good? They nearly always fail in one or more of the respects I have mentioned. The drumming is too loud or insensitive: one or more of the players is an exhibitionist; there is limited evidence of teamwork; amplification is allowed to unbalance the band and distort sounds,.... and so on.

On a related matter, I would like to quote from an email I received. It is from a gentleman who lives in Florida. He became a keen fan of Tuba Skinny after discovering the band early in 2015:

I have commented to others that Tuba Skinny is, in my humble opinion, the best trad jazz band in the world. Of course I haven't been exposed to every band in the world, but I haven't heard one better. Shaye forgoes what I call 'acrobatics' on the horn to play the actual music with her impeccable phrasing and reverence for the music. There is no show-off in her, trying to prove how facile she is on the cornet like many players, who only do so to the detriment of the music.

'FINGERING WITH YOUR FINGERS'

The tune *Fingering With Your Fingers* was created in 1935 by The Mississippi Sheiks. This string band was very active in the early 1930s, when they recorded about 70 tunes. The musicians were mostly members of the Chatmon family (living about 200 miles north of New Orleans and descended from slaves). The best-known member of the family was Armenter Chatmon, who used the stage name 'Bo Carter': he also had a solo career. In performance, there would be between three and five men in the group and the principal instruments were guitars and violin. Many of their recordings (though not this one) had vocals. It is very simple and repetitive (with a 32-bar AABA structure). It also uses a basic, straightforward chord sequence. The melody is reminiscent of the 1930 song *Exactly Like You* (composed by Jimmy McHugh and Dorothy Fields), though it has a quite different Middle Eight.

Practically nobody today would have been aware of this lively tune had it not been for the revival of it, in about 2012, by Tuba Skinny - and their frequent playing of it in public.

For example, to watch an exhilarating YouTube performance of *Fingering With Your Fingers* in 2013, type in 'Tuba Skinny Fingering with your Fingers Royal St. 4/13/13'. That was filmed for us by *digitalalexa*; and Tuba Skinny comprised nine players on that day. It shows what really great jazz musicians can make out of even the simplest material. I hope you enjoy the way those two outstanding reed players - Jonathan and Ewan - traded bars in the early part of the video.

And when I visited New Orleans three years later, I found Tuba Skinny still merrily beginning a set with the tune. Here's the video I made at the time. Type in 'Tuba Skinny:

Fingering With Your Fingers'. On this occasion, Tuba Skinny had a line-up of eight musicians - only four of whom had also appeared in the 2013 video.

TUBA SKINNY AND MEMPHIS MINNIE

Memphis Minnie was quite somebody. She could play the guitar and sing well. But she was also a composer of some fine early jazz tunes.

Her real name was Lizzie Douglas and she was born in the New Orleans suburb of Algiers in 1897. Her family later lived in Tennessee. As a child, she mastered the banjo and guitar. She took to busking in the Beale Street, Memphis, area when she was only a teenager, and she also toured with a circus. It was a hard life. She became a tough, street-wise young woman; and this toughness was reflected later in her singing and playing.

She married three times. Her second husband, Joe McCoy, was a fellow busker. They were talent-spotted and went on to make records for both Columbia and Vocalion.

It was at that time (when she was already more than 30 years old) that the publicists decided to call her 'Memphis Minnie' and the name stuck. (Similarly, her husband was given the name 'Kansas Joe'.) Between 1929 and 1934, they recorded about 30 songs, some of them more than once. After they divorced, she recorded many more, sometimes with Kansas Joe's brother and later with her third husband - Ernest Lawler ('Little Son Joe'). At this time she was mainly based in Chicago.

Minnie recorded more than 130 songs in total, several of them composed by herself. Among songs Minnie recorded that have influenced and been revived by the young New Orleans musicians of the 21st Century are: *Bumble Bee, Frisco Town, I'm Goin' Back Home, Me and My Chauffeur, Ice Man, Tricks Ain't Walkin' No More, What's The Matter With the Mill?, New Dirty Dozen*, and *When the Levee Breaks*.

Minnie is known to have been the composer of the following songs that she recorded: *Black Cat Blues, You Caught Me Wrong Again, Down in the Alley, Good Biscuits, Good Morning, Has Anyone Seen My Man?, Hoodoo Lady, I Hate To See The Sun Go Down, I'm a Bad Luck Woman, I've Been Treated Wrong, Ice Man, If You See My Rooster, Keep On Eating, Ma Rainey, Man You Won't Give Me No Money, My Baby Don't Want Me No More, My Butcher Man, My Strange Man, Nothin' In Rambling*. Some of the other songs for which she became well known (such as *Bumble Bee* and *Me and My Chauffeur*) were written by McCoy or Lawler.

You can hear Minnie and her third husband (the composer) performing *Me and My Chauffeur* on YouTube by typing in 'Memphis Minnie - Me And My Chauffeur Blues'.

To watch Tuba Skinny performing this song, type in 'Tuba Skinny – Me and My Chauffeur 8/5/12 Rhinebeck Market'.

Memphis Minnie seems to have been the composer of *Frisco Town* (a ten-bar blues) in 1929. She recorded it with her husband Kansas Joe the same year. Its title rapidly changed to *Frisco Bound*. (This a quite different song from the *Frisco Bound* composed by Sam Powers in 1915.) Also in 1929, a recording of *Frisco Bound* was made by James Wiggins and this increased its popularity.

On YouTube, you can find Tuba Skinny performing *Frisco Bound* by typing in 'Tuba Skinny – Frisco Bound – Royal St. 4/12/13'.
In another video of Tuba Skinny, the young musicians may be seen performing one of the 12-bar blues written by Minnie's second husband (Joe McCoy). Enjoy especially at 2 mins 20 seconds (and again later) the descending triplets played by the clarinettist (Craig Flory) in his 'solo' chorus. The song is

called *If You Take Me Back*. You can watch the video filmed by *RaoulDuke504* by typing in 'Tuba Skinny If You Take Me Back'.

FROM 'CALL OF THE FREAKS' TO 'GARBAGE MAN'

'Take out your can! Here comes the Garbage Man!'

I have enjoyed this song ever since I first heard it in 2012. It's simple, catchy and requires only the singing of the above words three times over a basic 12-bar blues.

However, having got round to studying the tune and writing it out (by ear) today, I discovered it has quite a history.

Originally it was 'Call of the Freaks', recorded in 1929 by both the Luis Russell Orchestra and the King Oliver Orchestra. I am uncertain who composed it. Possibly it was King Oliver (perhaps collaborating with Dave Nelson) or more probably it was Luis Russell.

Within a year or two, it was recorded by the Luis Russell band as 'New Call of the Freaks', said to be by Russell's percussionist, Paul Barbarin. In fact, I can't detect much that is 'new' about this version.

However, at about this time it acquired the 'Garbage Man' vocal chorus mentioned above. Then it caught on with vaudeville-type singers, such as *Milton Brown and his Musical Brownies*. By now, it was renamed 'Garbage Man Blues'.

A further stage (in my opinion one we could have done without) involved a few singers thinking it funny to add scatological lyrics.

But in its latest manifestation - performed by Tuba Skinny - it is simple, infectious, innocuous and pure fun.

To enjoy it, go to YouTube and type 'Tuba Skinny – Garbage Man – Spotted Cat 4-10-12'. This should take you to a delightful recording made by that most prolific and generous video-maker, *digitalalexa*. This was in the days when the band included Jonathan, Ewan and Ryan.

There's much that makes this piece appealing. Best played at a tempo of crotchet = 150, it begins by vamping two bars.

They can be repeated anything from four to eight times. Then there can be some solo choruses - either 12-bars or 16 bars (over the continued vamping of the above bars). Then we have a little bridge that leads into the 12-bar blues, with the 'Take out your can' vocal.

Following this, the 12-bar blues pattern may be repeated *ad lib*; but a good coda is provided if the band plays the 'bridge' again to finish.

On their 2017 CD, 'Tupelo Pines', Tuba Skinny play this tune again, in a more sophisticated arrangement; and this time they have gone back to its earlier title 'Call of the Freaks'. I'm pleased to say they still include the 'Take out your can….' vocal.

'HE LIKES IT SLOW'

An Australian who introduced himself as relatively new to traditional jazz emailed to ask me whether I could offer any help with *He Likes It Slow* (by W. Benton Overstreet), which he was having difficulty in picking up, having heard it played by Tuba Skinny. Like many who write to me, he overestimated my powers!

However, I would suggest first going back (as Tuba Skinny must have done) to the 1926 recording featuring Butterbeans and Susie and Louis Armstrong. Type in YouTube 'Louis Armstrong – He Like It Slow (1926)'. It is remarkably clear for a recording of such a vintage.

There's a simple Introduction and then a twelve-bar Verse, which is followed by a 20-bar (+2-bar tag) Chorus (with a 'break' on bars 7 - 8) making strong use of *The Salty Dog Chord Progression*. Note also how the band does a double-speed version of the first half of the Chorus as an interlude.

Tuba Skinny offer us a recording of this song on their CD *Six Feet Down* (made in 2010) and they are also seen performing it in several videos on YouTube, such as the one you may access by typing in 'Tuba Skinny at Wild Hive Farm on 9/5/2010 He Likes It Slow'. (Incidentally, they offer a full two choruses at the double tempo.)

The original Armstrong recording of 1926 was in the key of F. Tuba Skinny happily and brilliantly tackle it in Eb. The key suits Erika's voice perfectly, which is probably why they opted for it.

However, when Shaye (this time on piano) and Erika (singing) recorded the song again as a trio in a run-of-the-mill performance with Norbert Susemihl on trumpet, they played it in the key of F. I wonder why. This version is also available on YouTube.

'HILARITY RAG'

When I was in New Orleans during April 2016, as I mentioned when writing about Robin Rapuzzi, I had the good fortune to be in Royal Street while Tuba Skinny were busking. Their programme included *Hilarity Rag*. Apparently this was a tune they had only just learned and they were giving their first public performance of it. I managed to film it. You can see and hear the video on YouTube by typing in 'Tuba Skinny Hilarity Rag'. This should bring you to: https://www.youtube.com/watch?v=BvBxfc2jHb0.

But where does *Hilarity Rag* come from? The answer is that it was composed in 1910 - an early piano rag by James Scott (who also wrote such classics *Climax Rag*, *Ophelia Rag* and *Grace and Beauty*).

You can find on YouTube the original piano rag (and see the sheet music - with sincere thanks to the video-maker codenamed *RagtimeDorianHenry*).

Like so many of those early piano rags, it had to be 'simplified' and adapted quite a bit to make it playable as a full-band piece. Bunk Johnson obviously liked it and played it with his bands. Fortunately, at the end of his revived career, he was recorded in New York, playing his version. If you listen to it, you will find it sounds quite a bit different from the piano piece.

Other bands before Tuba Skinny have taken it up from there. For example, there's a lovely clear performance by an English band with the late Norman Thatcher on trumpet. You can also find that on YouTube. It is at: https://www.youtube.com/watch?v=GPEBV_7JIKQ.

I remember Norman Thatcher as one of the rare musicians who also had Scott's *Grace and Beauty* in his repertoire in the 1980s.

Tuba Skinny's version closely follows the Bunk Johnson reinterpretation of Scott's original.

I must mention that they also added to their repertoire in April 2016 tunes called *Frog Hop* and *Frog-i-More Rag*. Unfortunately I did not video them playing these tunes. But I noted that *RaoulDuke504* did so in the weeks that followed, so you may care to seek out his videos of them playing those tunes. Clifford Hayes composed *Frog Hop* in 1929 and recorded it with his Louisville Stompers. Tuba Skinny's version, that I heard them play at the dba in New Orleans on 8 April 2016, was modelled very closely on this - including the sustained link notes at the ends of choruses.

Frog-i-More Rag is, of course, a much better known piece - in the repertoire of most bands. It was composed by Jelly Roll Morton in 1918.

'I'M BLUE AND LONESOME'

I received this email from a gentleman in England:
I've just been listening to the 3 recordings on YouTube of Tuba Skinny playing 'Blue and Lonesome'. All are good but the one that thrills me most is played on Royal Street 4/11/14 on digitalalexa. Erika's singing and the instrumental work are in perfect sympathy. They caress the melody and play both individually and collectively in the best New Orleans tradition. How do they do it so well? I've now listened to several of the other New Orleans busking groups and there isn't one, including those involving some of the regular TS musicians, which comes within a mile of what they achieve. Wonderful, wonderful jazz. What a find.

There seem to have been several tunes with the title 'Blue and Lonesome'; but the one Tuba Skinny have featured, with Erika Lewis singing, is the song composed probably in the late 1930s by the singer Georgia White and her pianist Richard M. Jones.

It is a fine song to add to the repertoire of any band with a good singer. And it is somewhat unusual in being a 24-bar tune, so it makes a welcome change from those with a conventional 32-bar a-a-b-a structure.

In fact, I am struggling at the moment to think of other 24-bar tunes performed by traditional jazz bands (apart from 12-bar blues with two themes, which don't really count, and *Midnight in Moscow*, which is really a 16-bar tune with the second eight repeated). The Chorus of *Over in the Gloryland* comprises 24 bars. So does the Chorus of *Sing On*, and the Chorus of *Tailgate Ramble*. Also, there was a fashion in the first two decades of the Twentieth Century for songs that had VERSES of 24 bars, even if the better-known CHORUS had 32 bars. Examples are *San* and *I'm Forever Blowing Bubbles*.

For an indoor performance (this is quite something!), with Shaye on piano rather than cornet, type in YouTube 'Tuba Skinny & Shaye Cohn – Piano – Blue and Lonesome – Spotted Cat'. This will take you to another of *digitalalexa*'s fine videos. It's fairly simple tune to play along with, so if you care to try, note that they are in the key of G.

'JACKSON STOMP' AND 'CROW JANE'

Here's something surprising - a tune comprising ELEVEN bars (measures).

I am acquainted with perhaps a thousand tunes played by traditional jazz bands, but virtually all the tunes contain multiples of four bars. Most common are the 12-bar blues and 32-bar standards.

In all those hundreds of tunes, the only one made up of eleven bars is *Jackson Stomp*.

Musicians feel, think and play the music in four-bar phrases.

So eleven should not work! And yet *Jackson Stomp* really has eleven bars. When I first noticed this, I could not believe my ears. Had I miscounted? I checked and re-checked.

It felt like a 12-bar blues but sure enough it really was complete after 11 bars.

I found out that it originated with *Cow Cow Blues*, written and recorded in 1928 by Cow Cow Davenport. You can hear this on YouTube. In this form, it was a standard 12-bar, played in boogie woogie style.

But the tune was taken up by Charles McCoy ('Papa Charlie'), who lived from 1909 to 1950. He slightly adapted it into *Jackson Stomp* and recorded it with his colleague Bo Carter in *The Mississippi Mud Steppers*. It was at this point that it became the tune of eleven bars.

They also recorded it again (this time eleven bars with lyrics) as *The Lonesome Train That Carried My Girl Away*.

Now how is it possible for an 11-bar tune to sound right? What is the trick?

I'm not sure that I have the answer, but let me try.

Take the chords of a 12-bar as (at their most basic):

I I I I IV IV I I V V I I

We find that *Jackson Stomp* IS essentially a 12-bar, but with the clever twist of omitting Bar 9.

I I I I IV IV I I V I I

To watch Tuba Skinny play it, go to YouTube and type in 'Tuba Skinny Jackson Stomp Royal St. 4/12/13'.

Tuba Skinny play it in Bb. They sail through it, chorus after chorus, with their usual brilliant collective improvisations, as if an eleven-bar song was the most natural thing in the world. (Unusually - and this is another illustration of the band's versatility - on their CD 'Rag Band' they even recorded it without trombone or cornet: Shaye switched to violin.)

And what about *Crow Jane*? I had never heard of this song before Tuba Skinny introduced me to it. Apparently it was made up and recorded by Nehemiah 'Skip' James 90 years ago.

The tricky thing about this number is that, although it is basically a repetitive eight-bar tune, it also has an optional 2-bar tag.

Tuba Skinny deal with this tag in different ways in their various YouTube performances. On the 'Rag Band' CD, they choose to have the band playing four choruses of eight bars, then Erika singing five choruses in 10-bar form - apart from the penultimate, which she takes as 8 bars. The band then plays more eight-bar choruses, Erika returns with some ten-bars, and the band rounds things off with choruses of eight bars; and yet there is one more twist: a TWELVE-bar chorus (including a four-bar tag) to finish. Sounds complicated? Yes. But such is the discipline and understanding within this band that nobody trips up, nobody puts a foot wrong. They play it as one. And, as usual, the improvisations on the basic theme are mind-boggling.

'LATE HOUR BLUES', 'MEMPHIS SHAKE' AND 'MICHIGANDER BLUES'

In 2015 Tuba Skinny introduced into their repertoire yet another of those simple, bouncy 16-bar tunes (essentially 8 + 8) that have catchy themes and are easy to play because they hardly need more than three basic chords. The song is *Late Hour Blues*.

Written by the New Orleans-born pianist Richard M. Jones in 1939, it was recorded by Georgia White for Decca (the company for which Richard Jones was a record producer at the time). It was Decca's catalogue number 7741B (65756).

Described on the Decca label as 'Blues Singing With Orchestra' *Late Hour Blues* has Georgia White alternating 16-bar choruses with members of the 'orchestra', which seems to comprise percussion, a very fluent cornet, a clarinet, guitar (Lonnie Johnson?) and piano (Richard Jones?). Vocals alternate on the 16-bar theme with instrumental 16-bar solos. It seems to work on a familiar chord pattern:
IV - IV - I - I - V7 - Vdim - V7 - V7 - IV - IV - I - I - V7 - V7 - I - I.

Tuba Skinny take the song briskly in Bb. They make a great job of it. Like Georgia White, Erika sings choruses between instrumental solos. Georgia sings four 16-bar choruses; Erika sings five. The final two are sung without an instrumental break. They appropriately include the 'Oh Me! Oh My!' Chorus for a second time - thereby achieving the five choruses in all. Enjoy the video made by *digitalalexa* of Tuba Skinny performing this song by typing in YouTube 'Tuba Skinny Late Hour Blues LMF 4/14/15'.

There is a terrific video of Tuba Skinny performing *Memphis Shake*. It is expertly filmed; and the tune is brilliantly played. Unfortunately the start of the tune was not caught; but I think it's a video you would enjoy. You can find it (not on YouTube but on Vimeo) by going to: https://vimeo.com/81591425.

This tune was recorded in 1926 by a group known as *The Dixieland Jug Blowers* in Chicago. Though called a 'jug' band, they had such instruments as trombone, piano and saxophone in their line-up. What made their recording of 'Memphis Shake' special was that the great clarinettist Johnny Dodds was sitting in with them, and his contribution is very effective on the old recording. (You can find it on YouTube.)

Not much is known about *The Dixieland Jug Blowers*. It seems to have been a short-term amalgamation of two early 'jug' bands - run respectively by old-timer Earle McDonald (banjo and jug) and Clifford Hayes (violin). It is believed that Clifford Hayes was the composer of 'Memphis Shake'.

Actually, it's not so much a tune as a simple sequence of chords that are an effective basis for improvisation. The tune has a four-bar introduction and then is in two parts.

The most distinctive feature of the chords is the repeated use of two bars on the diminished tonic. These give 'Memphis Shake' its particular flavour.

Part B of the tune - with the 4-beat notes over the first four bars (during which the banjo can indulge in some luscious tremolos), provides a good contrast with the bulk of the tune and improvisations, which are based on Part A.

There is also a YouTube video of Tuba Skinny making a

great job of this tune. Enjoy it by typing in 'Tuba Skinny Memphis Shake LMF 4/14/15'.

Michigander Blues was apparently written in about 1929 by Jabbo Smith and the word 'Michigander' simply means 'a person from Michigan'.

To hear Tuba Skinny on YouTube perform *Michigander Blues*, type in 'Tuba Skinny Michigander Blues Spotted Cat 4/10/12'.

It is an unusual and distinctive piece, exploiting the minor key (D minor, in fact). The first four bars are the Introduction; the next 16 bars are the Verse; and the rest (final 32 bars) are the CHORUS, which has an a-a-b-a structure. Tuba Skinny make the most of opportunities for various instruments to take the lead on 8-bar chunks of the Chorus.

'NEED A LITTLE SUGAR IN MY BOWL'

The amazing Dick Baker has spent decades researching the origins and histories of tunes played by traditional jazz bands. He now has information about nearly 4000 tunes on his website, which runs to over 400 pages of closely-typed information. Go to http://dickbaker.org/ and then select *Stomp Off Records Project*.

Dick has been tracing the origins of *I Need A Little Sugar In My Bowl*, the song made famous by Bessie Smith and brilliantly revived by Tuba Skinny and Erika Lewis.

Try going to YouTube and typing in 'Tuba Skinny and his Tiny Men (sugar in my bowl)'. You will find the tune is concise (only 30 bars in total) and therefore simple for musicians to learn and memorise. It has a good, strong, easily-singable melody and a very pleasant down-the-ladder harmonic progression (plus *The Sunshine Chord Sequence* at the end). Bars 7 and 8 of the Chorus can be played as a 'Break' - to be taken either by a singer or by one of the instruments; and Bars 17 and 18 of the Chorus are an appealing 'Tag'. For all these reasons, *I Need A Little Sugar In My Bowl* is a very good tune for jazz bands to have in their repertoire.

Dick Baker sent me an email:
In my quest to update and improve the Stomp Off Index, I went hunting for this on a trip to the Library of Congress in January. The composers were actually Dally Small, Clarence Williams and J. Tim Brymn, and the filed copyright was "I Want a Little Sugar in My Bowl." The original lead sheet, possibly in Clarence Williams's handwriting, is available. The copyright as printed in the book reads 'I need a little sugar in my bowl words and melody by C. Williams, Dally Small and J. T. Brymn. © 1 c.

Jan. 14, 1932; E unp. 50141; Clarence Williams music pub. co., inc., New York'. The record label, alas, screwed things up a bit. The initial "I" was dropped (but it's common for record companies to shorten, streamline, or otherwise change titles for their labels), but the composer credit on the Columbia 14634-D label is Williams, Byrne [or poss. Byrns] and Small. There WAS a composer named W. A. D. "Danny" Small, but this evidently isn't that guy.

The lead-sheet Dick looked at is dated (by rubber stamp) '1932'. It has a melody line and no chords for the Chorus and a melody line and a few hints at chords for the Verse. The Verse has 16 bars. The Chorus has 18 bars (really 16 bars plus a two-bar tag).

The 16-bar Verse is typical of its time - not specially interesting melodically, simple and with a repeated phrase, and ending with a dominant 7th to lead into the Chorus.

What I find strange is that Bessie Smith recorded it (in a musically very good version) in 1931; and yet the copyright manuscript (not such good music - especially the Verse) is dated 1932. I would have expected it to be the other way round.

Bessie Smith sang a shorter (12-bar) verse which is better than the 16-bar Verse in that manuscript. Turning to the Chorus, Bessie's version is very close to the manuscript version of the melody. Bessie, by the way, sang the song in the key of F, though the manuscript is in Ab.

When Tuba Skinny recorded the song (on their first CD, in May 2009), they based their performance on the Bessie Smith version, including the 12-bar Verse and using the key of F.

With regard to the lyrics Dick Baker discovered, Bessie Smith kept close to the first three lines of the Verse, but scrapped the remaining three, replacing them with one line (thereby reducing the Verse to 12 bars). In the Chorus, Bessie pretty well kept the words as in the manuscript, though she slightly amended a couple of phrases.

Bessie then went on to sing a second Chorus (not typed into the manuscript). This second Chorus was based on the first, but with cruder metaphors.

I'm pleased Tuba Skinny's version omits Bessie's second Chorus altogether. Erika Lewis sings the Verse and first Chorus only, following Bessie Smith but with a little toning down of the language, conveying a mood rather than archness. And Tuba Skinny abbreviates the title even further to *Need a Little Sugar*.

Writers of jazz history books in the past used to snigger like schoolboys at the 'innuendos' in the lyrics of songs performed by the likes of Bessie Smith, Victoria Spivey and Lucille Bogan. (In England, we had the songs of George Formby: their 'cheekiness' was fashionable at one time.) But we live in an age when people are neither amused nor shocked by the metaphors used; and today I think there is little appetite for this kind of verbal humour.

So, regardless of the lyrics, let us value this tune for its conveying of mood, its conciseness, its simplicity, its strong melody, its harmonic progression, its 'Break' and its 'Tag'.

'OWL CALL BLUES'

In 2014, Tuba Skinny created a beautiful slow-paced song, *Owl Call Blues*. It is gloriously sung by Erika Lewis. The melody was written by Shaye Cohn and the lyrics by Erika herself. What a team! As I mentioned earlier, it is included it on their sixth CD, which is actually called *Owl Call Blues* and contains 14 other tunes, such as *Dallas Rag* and *Oriental Strut*.

I can tell you this haunting, melancholy tune immediately embeds itself in your mind. You will want to hear it again and again; and you will go around humming it for days.

It's not a 12-bar blues. It is a 16-bar tune that begins by working its way down a chromatic ladder of long notes. In general feel, it has something in common with Jelly Roll Morton's 1938 composition, *Sweet Substitute*, Fred Meinken's *Wabash Blues* (of 1921) and Alex Hill's 1934 song *Delta Bound* (which Tuba Skinny have also brilliantly recorded).

Tuba Skinny perform it entirely in Bb.

Erika's lyrics comprise two 8-line verses of mystic wistful, nostalgic, pastoral poetry. Both verses begin with the same four lines, but the second four lines are different.

If, like me, you can't resist trying to play along with it yourself, you will probably be able to pick out both the melody and the chord structure. In the main it seems to be a three-chorder, though for the long note (E) - in Bars 3 and 4 - I settled on Bb diminished.

I first came across this tune in two YouTube videos by the video-maker *digitalalexa*. One was recorded inside a museum and the acoustic is inevitably resonating, bringing out the full glory of Erika's voice. The Band (with Shaye going for the higher octave) plays three choruses before Erika sings. Find it on YouTube by typing in 'Tuba Skinny Owl Call Blues Ogden Museum 4/17/14'.

The second, filmed in the open air , obviously has a quite different acoustic. You can watch it by typing in 'Tuba Skinny Owl Call Blues Royal St 4/18/14'.

'ORIENTAL STRUT'

An appearance on YouTube of Tuba Skinny playing *Oriental Strut* (in YouTube type in 'Oriental Strut Tuba Skinny 2015' to find it) prompted me to give some thought to this tune, which is a little more complex than most, and not easy to play.

It was written in 1926 by Johnny St. Cyr and famously recorded that year by Louis Armstrong and His Hot Five (with St. Cyr himself on banjo).

Tuba Skinny take it at a slightly quicker pace than Armstrong. Their performance lasts for 3 minutes 13 seconds (about 4 seconds longer than Armstrong's) but with Tuba Skinny you get 32 more bars.

It may be heresy to say so, but - as an arrangement - I prefer Tuba Skinny's to Armstrong's.

The key for Tuba Skinny is F (and the related key D minor). The Armstrong version today sounds (very improbably) in E, but I think 90 years ago the standard pitch was different; so he was most likely also playing it in F (D minor).

Tuba Skinny differs from Armstrong in going back to play Themes A and B again - after two choruses of Theme C. Also Shaye Cohn chooses to play only 16 bars against stop chords in her 'solo', whereas Armstrong plays the full 32 bars - not sharing with another player.

Here is an analysis of the two versions.

<u>Introduction</u>: The Hot Five offer 4 bars clearly establishing the minor key; followed by 4 bars – piano – vamping on the minor key. Tuba Skinny do the same, except that they are tuba-led in the vamping.

Theme A: The Hot Five play the 16 bars strongly the minor, with a vamp (piano) at Bars 7 – 8. Tuba Skinny play the 16 bars strongly on D minor.

Theme B: Both bands play these 16 bars - brighter because now in the related major key of F. *The Salty Dog Chord Sequence* is used, ending on the chord of C7 to lead neatly into Theme C.

Theme C: The Hot Five plays the 32-bar Main Theme. Trombone leads on first 16 bars, clarinet the next 16. The banjo provides a 2-bar link in bars 31-32 (the composer's chance to shine!). With Tuba Skinny, the trombone leads on all 32 bars, - but with backing from cornet and clarinet in the final 16.

Theme C (played again): The 32 bars are Louis's solo and chance to shine against stop chords. But the whole band joins in at the final eight. With Tuba Skinny, the clarinet takes a sprightly lead.

Theme C (played again): The Hot Five play it again, but with Louis's cornet dominating (and Johnny St. Cyr again taking a two-bar break – this time at bars 15-16). Tuba Skinny spring a surprise: they play Themes A and B instead - Theme A: 16 bars in D minor, with the tuba taking the first eight and the full ensemble the next eight. Theme B: 16 bars in F played ensemble but ending with a washboard two-bar offbeat break.

Ending: The Hot Five provide a very pleasant rallentando coda of just two bars. But Tuba Skinny are not ready to finish just yet. They play Theme C – the 32-bar Main Theme in F. This is Shaye's solo against stop chords, but unlike Louis she chooses to play only the first 16 bars in this way. We then have the washboard for 8 bars against dotted crotchet double stop chords, and the whole band back in for the final 8 bars. To round the performance off, there is a two-bar tag, with no rallentando, and a neat 'chopped' ending.

What a performance!

'POSTAGE STOMP'

It is always a joy to hear an up-tempo tune played with real energy and drive, and with a total sense of control and great teamwork. It is an experience that, I'm sorry to say, does not happen often enough here in England. So many of our musicians are very elderly and are really not up to producing that drive any more. (I am one of them!)

If you look at a performance given on 30 March 2016 by Tuba Skinny, filmed by the Louisiana-based video-maker *RaoulDuke504*, you will see what we are failing to achieve. In YouTube, type 'Tuba Skinny – Postage Stomp' to find it.

They are giving a routine street performance of *Postage Stomp*. It's a bright, chirpy, conventional 32-bar tune with a simple familiar chord pattern - very similar to that of *Has Anybody Seen My Girl?* Its Middle Eight (as in dozens of other tunes) appears to be:
 III7 - III7 - VI7 - VI7 - II7 - II7 - V7 - V7
This allows for 'breaks' in Bars 23/24. So it's an easy tune to pick up and improvise on.

Barnabus, the regular trombone player, is absent, but one chorus is taken by the saxophone and, in the first half of another chorus, the cornet and clarinet trade fours. Further variety is provided by a percussion chorus (against stop chords) and a tuba-led chorus - with the clarinet, sax and cornet playing long notes to decorate the Middle Eight. Above all, though, four of the choruses involve dramatic, driving work from the full ensemble. There is brightness and energy from all quarters, with Robin on percussion and Shaye, so busy on cornet, never allowing the tempo or the excitement to drop. The banjo, guitar, tuba and drums keep the tune pounding along in rock-steady fashion.

For Tuba Skinny, this performance was probably nothing special - just another day at the office. But for elderly gents such as myself who are struggling to play the music, it's an object lesson.

Postage Stomp is a tune from 1930, featured that year by Maynard Baird and His Orchestra. You can also find their bouncing, slickly-arranged version on YouTube.

Maynard Baird's 'Orchestra' - an obscure but very smooth outfit - was based in Knoxville, Tennessee; and in April 1930 *Postage Stomp* was one of two tunes they recorded for the Vocalion label. I have been unable to discover beyond doubt who composed it. One source gives 'Goebel and Johnston'. So it seems a very reasonable inference that they were Sam Goble and Vic Johnston - trumpet player and pianist respectively in Baird's band.

In the Baird recording, impressive performances are given by Buddy Thayer on banjo, Harold Taft on baritone saxophone, Horace Ogle on trombone and Ebb Grubb on sousaphone. But the whole presentation is polished, using a well-crafted written arrangement that treats the 32-bar theme in a variety of ways. Maynard Baird (who appears to have been the conductor and leader) chose to pitch the tune rather high - in the key of F, whereas Tuba Skinny opted for the more comfortable Bb.

And, while we are on the subject of playing with energy and drive, seek out Tuba Skinny (in the same set as *Postage Stomp*), playing *Dallas Rag*. Sensational!

'PYRAMID STRUT'

Tuba Skinny's fifth CD - *Pyramid Strut* - is available for digital download. All you need to do to download is this. Go to https://tubaskinny.bandcamp.com/album/pyramid-strut and follow the instructions. You can pay for it easily (e.g. by PayPal) even if you do not live in the USA. You can even listen on line before you buy.

This CD was recorded in Tasmania during the band's Australian tour in 2013 and in my opinion is their best. It has excellent sound quality and of course the technical standard the musicians had reached by 2013 was so high that this CD is truly outstanding.

Talking about it, washboard-player Robin Rapuzzi said: *Recording 'Pyramid Strut' was far different from any recording experience I think any of us will ever have again, as the space in which we recorded was very beautiful and sacred. A man named Chris Townsend had us over to his home outside of Hobart in the middle of Virgin Tassie Forest. He welcomed us and let us camp out on his property in some old fruit-picker shacks as well as recorded the album in its entirety. It was a pleasure to work with him and get to know his style. Normally we just record our music at home with blankets hung on the wall or a mattress leaned up against a corner to act as a sound barrier. I'm sure the sheer beauty of jungle around influenced us, as well as having the time and space to do it. Often when we record, we don't give ourselves that much time to get the job done and it can feel rushed. In Tassie, we recorded I think it was over 20 tracks the first day and a similar amount the following day. Recording on that property allowed us to discuss a lot of everything and everyone's own ideas about the album.*

15 tracks were eventually used on the CD, including such gems as *Alligator Crawl*, *Deep Henderson* and *Big Chief*

Battleaxe. The polished, disciplined performances are stunning. There is also some terrific singing from Erika in such numbers as *Slow Drivin' Moan* (in a great arrangement making good use of Barnabus's trombone) and in *Lonesome Drag*, for which she wrote the lyrics. Here's the full list:

Big Chief Battle Axe
Lonesome Drag
Freight Train Blues (Lorraine Walton composition from 1938)
Pyramid Strut
I Got The Cryin' Blues
Cold Morning Shout
Hesitation Blues
Skid Dat De Dat
Mean Blue Spirits
You've Got To Give Me Some
Sweet Lovin' Old Soul
Alligator Crawl
Blood Thirsty Blues
Deep Henderson
Slow Drivin' Moan

May I draw your attention especially to the eponymous *Pyramid Strut*, an amazing composition by Shaye Cohn, who also plays a prominent part in its performance? This is a complex Mortonesque piece. In fact it's in the spirit of such tunes as *Red Hot Peppers Stomp*, recorded by Morton and His Red Hot Peppers in 1928.

Pyramid Strut begins in the Key of Eb. It has a 4-bar Introduction which in other contexts could be mistaken for the final four bars of a tune. It runs down the scale of Eb in the third bar and so establishes the key. Then we have a first theme consisting of 24 bars and played twice. Bars 1, 5 and 21 contain a distinctive little phrase (a minim each on A and Bb) which give this theme a special character. But its other notable feature is that Bars 17 to 20 inclusive are played as 'Breaks' (exactly what Morton would have approved of). The first time this theme is played, the cornet takes the lead and also the breaks; the second time the clarinet.

Then the tune moves immediately and energetically into a second theme. This consists of 12 bars on the basic 12-bar blues chord pattern. As you may know, it was also a common practice in the 1920s to slot a 12-bar blues theme into the middle of structured compositions. (Think of *The Chant*, for example.) Shaye's 12-bar theme is played through twice - first vigorously stated by the cornet and secondly with the full ensemble. We are still in the key of Eb.

Straight into the third theme we then go; and we find ourselves now in the key of Ab. What we have here is a 16-bar theme and this too is played twice. But what a tricky theme! In each set of 16 bars, bars 1 and 2, bars 3 and 4, bars 9 and 10 and bars 11 and 12 are taken as breaks! That gives you four breaks in 16 bars - twice; so eight breaks in all. On the recording, the eight breaks are taken respectively by cornet, clarinet, trombone, tuba, cornet, cornet, cornet and cornet.

This is followed by an attractive 8-bar Bridge passage, which is extraordinary because it teasingly plays around (if my ear serves me correctly) on the F minor arpeggio. But the Bridge ends by running down through the Eb7 chord which of course leads us back beautifully into Ab. This will remain the key of the fourth (and final) theme.

This fourth theme consists of 16 bars on a simple chord sequence. It is played three times. The clarinet leads us through it the first time, playing a tricky melody almost entirely of semi-quavers. Next, the banjo and tuba take the lead (a nice touch) for the second 16-bar chorus. Finally the whole band joins in for a climactic ensemble improvising over the 16 bars. And there's one more (Mortonesque) cheeky surprise: in a brief coda, those two minims from the opening theme bring the piece to an end, rounding it off perfectly. But this time (because the key has changed to Ab) they are played on the notes D and Eb.

Wow! I feel exhausted simply writing about it. Listen carefully to this piece. You will love it. Admire the discipline, the tightness of the playing and the technique of all seven players. You are witnessing what will come to be seen as one of the masterpieces of recorded jazz history.

What a talented lady Shaye Cohn is! (By the way, she even did the extraordinarily detailed and painstaking artwork on the CD cover.)

Also note especially Shaye's busy playing on *Big Chief Battleaxe*. She can take a simple theme and create so much out of it, whether soloing or supporting the other players.

Aren't we lucky to be able - all over the world - to enjoy the fruits of her marvellous composing, arranging and playing?

'SALAMANCA BLUES'

Salamanca Blues can be heard on Tuba Skinny's 2012 CD 'Rag Band'. It was composed by Shaye Cohn. As performed on the CD, it is a short, unpretentious, medium-tempo, charming and melodic piece, without a vocal. The whole thing is over in less than three minutes and it comprises just 76 bars (measures), which are made up of six segments:

1. 12-bar simple blues in F, firmly stated as a trombone solo by Barnabus Jones.

2. 16-bar soaring theme in F, just as firmly stated on Shaye's cornet - starting on the high F. There is some lovely tremolo support from the banjo and the harmonies are beautiful.

3. A key change! With no modulation, the full ensemble is straight and decisively led by the cornet into a 12-bar blues in Ab.

4. A second 12-bar ensemble in Ab.

5. Another 12-bar in Ab, this time stated by the banjo with (from Jonathan Doyle's clarinet) some cascading sweetness over a Db chord and also a two-bar solo 'break' - the only break in the 76 bars.

6. A final 12-bar ensemble blues chorus, again firmly started by Shaye on the high F - turning the chord into an Ab6. But, with a slight rallentando, all is brought to a calm neat ending.

Why did Shaye call her composition *Salamanca Blues*? I don't know. But my guess is it was named for Salamanca in Spain. Tuba Skinny have visited that country, though it seems Shaye may have composed the tune during a tour in Australia.

By the way, there is a YouTube video of Tuba Skinny playing this number. It begins at 3 minutes 22 seconds if you type in 'Tuba Skinny on Smart Arts Feb 2013'.

Better still, do what I did: buy the CD, which also contains such treats as *Jackson Stomp*, *Banjoreno* and *Russian Rag*.

'SKID DAT DE DAT'

Skid-Dat-De-Dat (sometimes spelled *Skit-Dat-De-Dat*) is a curiosity within the traditional jazz repertoire. You could describe it as a 'stop-start' tune because on six or more occasions the band stops playing and leaves one instrument alone to improvise a two-bar 'break'.

So this tune does not fit into any conventional pattern of composition: there's no 32-bar a-a-b-a or 12-bar blues structure to be spotted here.

Lil Hardin composed it in 1926 for her husband Louis Armstrong and his Hot Five to develop. Basically what she gave Louis was a 4-bar phrase, plus the idea of attaching two-bar breaks.

In the key of D, the four-bar phrase consists of four semibreves, rising through F sharp, G, B flat and D.

The two-bar 'break' seems to be normally played on the basis of the chord of D, or D minor.

The main 4-bar theme is mostly played with all the band harmonising through the long notes. But occasionally - for variety - the players may cut loose and improvise over those four chords.

Finally, there is a slightly different 4-bar chord sequence [G7 - G7 - D7 - D7] which may be used to give variety.

Regard these four little units of music as your building blocks. Put them together and there you have it - *Skid Dat De Dat*!

How does the tune turn out in performance? Well,

unfortunately, because most bands find it impossible to memorise a 'knitting pattern' for this tune, they tend to play (usually a shade too slowly) from a printed arrangement on music stands in front of them. The result can be laboured and stodgy.

But it can sound really good, as in the original Louis Armstrong performance, which runs for 3 minutes and 14 seconds. Here and there, Louis uses his voice for a few notes at a time ('scatting') as an alternative to his cornet.

A concise but exemplary performance is given on their CD 'Pyramid Strut' by Tuba Skinny. This version comprises just 46 bars in total and the recording lasts for only 96 seconds. But all you need is there. The 'break' is taken 7 times - by cornet, cornet, clarinet, trombone, tuba, banjo and cornet respectively. The piece is beautifully book-ended by the first and last cornet breaks. To bring the piece to a satisfactory conclusion, the whole band joins in on the final chord of the final break - an important point to note. This is a great way to tackle the tune.

As far as I know, there is only one YouTube video of Tuba Skinny playing this piece. It runs for about 140 seconds - longer than on the CD because extra breaks are given near the end of the piece to the clarinet and trombone.

This is well worth watching if you fancy studying *Skid-Dat-De-Dat*; or even if you just want to get the feel of the 'stop-start' nature of this curious tune. It was generously filmed by the video-maker codenamed *stolpe31* at Rapperswil in 2013. Type in 'Tuba Skinny – Skid-Dat-De-Dat Rapperswil 30 juni 2013'.

'SOMEBODY'S BEEN LOVING MY BABY'

I know very little about 'Document Records', though Wikipedia tells me the company was established in 1986 and still seems to be active, now based in Scotland. It is clear it has done a great service for jazz by rescuing from obscurity and re-issuing hundreds of recordings from the period 1900 to 1945.

It's also exciting to note how influential these old recordings have been on the young generation of great traditional jazz musicians - particularly in New Orleans. For example, Tuba Skinny manage to pick tunes out from the long lists of material that are perfectly suited to their style and to Erika's voice in particular.

On one of Document's CDs, there are eleven songs performed in the 1920s by Mandy Lee. What do we know about Mandy Lee? Who was she? It has been suggested that 'Mandy Lee' was just a name given to an artist (or even more than one artist - certainly it is difficult to be sure that all eleven songs are sung by the same voice). I suppose it's one of those mysteries never to be solved.

Tuba Skinny have taken on the song *Somebody's Been Lovin' My Baby*; and of course they perform it extremely well. They included it on their sixth CD (*Owl Call Blues* - released in August 2014). And you can watch them perform it (filmed for us by *digitalalexa*) by typing in 'Tuba Skinny Somebody Been Loving My Baby Ogden Museum 4/17/14'.

'TANGLED BLUES' AND 'THOUGHTS'

I first heard *Tangled Blues* when Tuba Skinny performed it at The Louisiana Music Factory on 14 April 2015. It was a brand-new composition by Shaye Cohn, with words by Erika Lewis. I thought it was a very pleasant tune, somewhat country-and-western in feel and played in the Key of F.

But something about it struck me as strange.

You form the impression that you are listening to one melody. But listen carefully and you find there are two separate tunes. Let's call them A and B. They have a lot in common. For example there are *motifs* such as one that occurs in both A and B (giving the piece that feeling of unity), which consists of two bars with one beat rest followed by three crotchets and a semibreve, all on the same note.

It occurs twice in A, played (I think) on the chord of F. It also occurs twice in B, but this time (I think) played on the Bb chord. So we begin to see what a clever 'tangle' Shaye has woven for us. Part A has a lyric and comprises 18 bars. How many tunes can you think of that consist of 18 bars (not counting tunes that are really 16 bars with a 2-bar tag, such as *Sister Kate*)? Can you think of *any*? I can't. So Shaye has played a clever trick here, too.

However, Part B is a conventional 32 bars but with no lyric.

Despite their similarity of 'feel', the two parts sound (to my ear, which may be misleading me) quite different in chord structure. It seems A starts with, and twice uses, the I - IV - V - I chord pattern whereas B starts on the V chord (dominant - C7th, followed of course by the tonic), of which it makes much use later.

The whole performance goes like this:

4-bar Introduction
18-bar A (Ensemble)
32-bar B (Cornet 16 + Ensemble 16)
18-bar A (Todd on Tuba playing the melody)
32-bar B (Clarinet 16 + ensemble 16 - trombone with melody)
18-bar A (the only occurrence of the vocal - sung by Erika)
32-bar B (Ensemble, cornet-led)

Total = 154 bars; performance time about 4 minutes 20 seconds.

What a clever, pretty and intricate tangle indeed! Well done, Shaye!

On YouTube there is a street performance filmed by *RaoulDuke*. Type in 'Tuba Skinny Tangled Blues'.

And another lovely original Tuba Skinny tune to appear on YouTube is *Thoughts*, composed by the band's percussionist Robin Rapuzzi. It is a tune of which he has every right to feel proud.

You can hear Tuba Skinny playing it by typing in 'Tuba Skinny Thoughts' (with thanks to *RaoulDuke504* for capturing the performance and alerting the world to it).

Thoughts is played wistfully, at a gentle tempo. When you first hear it, you can easily fall into the trap of thinking it has a standard 32-bar structure (A - A - B - A) because it begins like that and also it runs to 96 bars (measures) in total - which normally would suggest it's played through three times (3×32).

But listen carefully and you find it is a bit more complex. The initial tune seems to comprise 40 bars, not 32 (A - A - B - A - A).

The 'A' theme is of a pretty rocking and 'descending the ladder' type. And the 'B' theme seems to have a deliberate echo of 'Mood Indigo'.

But after these forty bars, something different happens. There is a 16-bar 'Interlude' (let's call it Theme 'C') which seems to me to be using the related minor key.

By the end of that, we have completed 56 bars. So, 40 bars to go? Presumably the Main Theme (A - A - B - A - A) to be played again? Well, yes, but not quite. What we get is A - A - (a strange) B - B – A. In these final 40 bars, the first sixteen (led by the clarinet) are indeed the same as the opening sixteen (Theme A twice). But then we have the first four bars only of the 'B' (*Mood Indigo*) theme followed by 4 leaping new bars of melody. Then the full 'B' (eight bars) again, but with a slightly different ending from the first time it was played.
88 bars completed. 8 to go. These 8 turn out to be a final run through of Theme 'A'.

So in total, the 8-bar theme 'A' has been played seven times. It lingers is your head and you will be humming it for the rest of the day.

Robin wrote this piece during the band's Summer 2015 tour. It was - as he puts it - at first planned as a tune for 'Squeaky Violin'! But, he says: 'Sure sounds a lot better when the band plays it'!

I hope we shall hear more of Robin's compositions in the future.

'TRICKS AIN'T WALKING NO MORE'

One thing that appeals to me about *Tricks Ain't Walking No More* is that is feels like a standard 12-bar blues and yet it is actually 16 bars (there's a kind of 4-bar tag). This blues was first recorded in 1930 by Lucille Bogan (better known later as Bessie Jackson) and it seems that she was also the composer.

As with so many tunes that have come to my attention in recent years, I first heard it on one of the CDs made by Tuba Skinny - in this case 'Rag Band'. But you can also see them performing it by going to YouTube and typing in 'Tuba Skinny – Tricks Ain't Walking French Quarter 4/15/12'. Erika Lewis's wonderful soulful voice is just right for the song.

The song was written during the Great Depression and its slang terms would have been immediately understood, heartfelt and meaningful. I'll leave you to work out what kind of people 'tricks' were.

THE REPERTOIRE

Although the band has been in existence for only ten years, it has built up an extraordinary repertoire so different from that of hundreds of other trad bands who go on playing the same old *Bill Bailey*, *All of Me* and *Muskrat Ramble* month in, month out.

Tuba Skinny's programmes mostly comprise exciting unfamiliar gems they have unearthed from the 1920s and 1930s (e.g. *New Orleans Bump*, *You Can Have My Husband*, *Cold Morning Shout*, *Forget Me Not Blues*, *Jackson Stomp*, *The Cotton Pickers' Rag*, *Deep Henderson*, *Banjoreno*, *Treasures Untold*, *Russian Rag*, *Oriental Strut*, *Minor Drag*, *Michigander Blues*, *In Harlem's Araby*, *Me and My Chauffeur*, *A Jazz Battle*, *Droppin' Shucks*, *Fourth Street Mess Around*, *Carpet Alley Breakdown*). The almost-forgotten artists whose music they have revived include Lucille Bogan, Bo Carter, Big Bill Broonzy, Sara Martin, Victoria Spivey, Memphis Minnie, Jabbo Smith, Skip James, Merline Johnson, Blind Boy Fuller, Hattie Hart, The Memphis Jug Band, The Tennessee Chocolate Drops, Clara Smith, The Dixieland Jug Blowers, The South Street Trio and The Mississippi Mud Steppers; and of course they also play tunes associated with the better-known, such as Ma Rainey, Bessie Smith, Fats Waller, Louis Armstrong and Jelly Roll Morton. They will surprise you by going to some unconventional sources for tunes they turn into exciting traditional jazz - sources such as Ray Charles and the 21st-century Australian original C. W. Stoneking.

With considerable effort, I struggled for months to maintain and constantly update (on my 'Enjoying Traditional Jazz' Blog) a list of the tunes played by Tuba Skinny that appeared on YouTube. Sometimes the video-maker was unable to give a tune's title and I also had difficulty in identifying it. In a few cases, I found it impossible.

However, I did my best and the following list contains nearly 300 tunes you can already hear Tuba Skinny playing mainly on YouTube. (And don't forget that by 2017 they had also released eight CDs.)

I think you will agree that to have mastered such a repertoire is a remarkable achievement. And you will notice how many of these wonderful tunes are missing from the repertoire of most trad bands.

After You've Gone (on their CD *Tuba Skinny*) (Creamer and Layton, 1927)
Ain't Gonna Give Nobody None of My Jelly Roll (Clarence & Spencer Williams, 1919; on their CD *Six Feet Down*)
Ain't That a Shame (Fats Domino and Dave Bartholomew, 1955)
All By Myself (Big Bill Broonzy, 1941. Up-tempo 12-bar blues)
Alligator Crawl (on their CD *Pyramid Strut*) (Fats Waller 1927)
All I Want is a Spoonful (Papa Charlie Jackson 8-bar theme from 1925)
Almost Afraid to Love (On their CD *Blue Chime Stomp*. Composed by Ann Turner for Georgia White, 1938)
Ambulance Man (Hattie Hart, 1930 ; on their CD *Owl Call Blues*)
Any Kinda Man (would be better than you) (on their CD *Garbage Man*. Recorded by Victoria Spivey, 1936)
Any Old Time (Jimmie Rodgers, 1929)
At The Jazz Band Ball (Nick La Rocca and Larry Shields, 1918; on their CD *Six Feet Down*)
Avalon (Da Sylva, Vincent Rose and Al Jolson, 1920; on their CD *Tuba Skinny*)

Baby, How Can It Be? (on their CD *Rag Band*) (Armenter Bo Chatmon [stage name Bo Carter] recorded it in 1931)
Baby, Please Don't Go (Joseph Lee 'Big Joe' Williams, 1935)
Ballin' The Jack (J. Burris and Chris Smith, 1923)
Banjoreno (on their CD *Rag Band*) (H. Clifford, 1926, for the Dixieland Jug Blowers)
Beautiful Dreamer (Stephen Foster, 1862. Probably the oldest tune in their repertoire)
Beer Garden Blues (Lewis Raymond and Clarence Williams, 1933, with words by Walter Bishop)
Bellamina (c. 1925. Anon. Bahaman folk song)
Big Chief Battleaxe (Composed by T. Allen in 1907; on their CD *Pyramid Strut*)
Bill Bailey (Hughie Cannon, 1909)
Billie's Blues (on their CD *Tuba Skinny*) (Billie Holiday, 1936)
Billy Goat Stomp (Jelly Roll Morton, 1927)
Biscuit Roller (on their CD *Rag Band*) (1937, Richard M. Jones and Georgia White)
Black Mountain Blues (J.C. Johnson, 1930. Recorded by Bessie Smith)
Blood Thirsty Blues (on their CD *Pyramid Strut*) (Written and recorded by Victoria Spivey, 1927)
Blue (Bill Mack, 1956)
Blue Chime Stomp (On their CD *Blue Chime Stomp*. Shaye Cohn, 2015)
Blue Devil Blues (possibly Sara Martin and her Jug Band 1925)
Blue Moon of Kentucky Keep on Shining (Bill Monroe, 1946)
Blues My Naughty Sweetie Gives to Me (Arthur Swanstone, Chas McCarron & Carey Morgan, 1919)
Bouncing Around (Armand J. Piron & Peter Bocage, 1923)
Broken-Hearted Blues (composed by Erika Lewis, 2009; on their CD *Tuba Skinny*; and on their CD *Blue Chime Stomp*.)
Broken-Hearted Blues (the second tune with this name - the one written and recorded by Lil Johnson in 1937 - is on their CD *Garbage Man*)

Bumblebee (recorded by Memphis Minnie in 1930)
Burgundy Street Blues (George Lewis, 1944. Shaye plays it on the cornet!)
Call of the Freaks (see also Garbage Man Blues.; on their CD *Tupelo Pine)*
Cannon Ball Blues (Jelly Roll Morton, 1926; on their CD *Owl Call Blues*)
Careless Love (on their CD *Tuba Skinny*) (W. C. Handy)
Carpet Alley Breakdown (Cal Smith and Henry Clifford. Recorded by Johnny Dodds, 1926)
C.C. (See See) Rider (Gertrude 'Ma' Rainey, 1925)
Cemetery Blues (Sid Laney, 1923. Recorded by Bessie Smith)
Chloe (C. N. Daniels and Gus Kahn, 1927. On their CD *Tuba Skinny*; and on their CD *Blue Chime Stomp.*)
Chocolate Avenue (on their CD *Tupelo Pine*; Clarence Williams, 1933)
Climax Rag (on their CD *Rag Band*) (James Scott, 1914)
Cold Mornin' Shout (on their CD *Pyramid Strut*) (Bobby Leecan for The South Street Trio, 1926)
Come On and Stomp Stomp Stomp (on their CD *Tupelo Pine;* Waller, Smith and Wells, 1927)
Cotton Pickers' Drag (Ben Tinnon, 1930, for the Grinnell Giggers)
Coquette (Guy Lombardo tune from 1928)
Corrine, What Makes You Treat Me So? (Blind Boy Fuller, 1937; 16-bar. On their CD *Blue Chime Stomp.*)
Crazy Blues (written by Perry Bradford, 1927)
Crazy 'Bout You (on their CD *Owl Call Blues*) (Big Bill Broonzy and the State Street Boys, 1935)
Crow Jane (on their CD *Rag Band*) (Skip James, 1931)
Crumpled Paper (Michael Magro, 2012. 12-bar in a minor key, played previously by Loose Marbles in the TV series 'Treme')
Dallas Blues (Hart A. Wand, 1912; words added by Lloyd Garrett, 1918)

Dallas Rag (on their CD *Owl Call Blues*; Dallas String Band, 1927)
Dangerous Blues (on their CD *Tupelo Pine;* ODJB 1921. Composed the the young girl Billie Brown, who died aged 18 of smallpox)
Dear Almanzoer (On their CD *Blue Chime Stomp*. Oscar 'Papa' Celestin, 1927)
Deep Bayou Moan (on their CD *Tupelo Pine*; Shaye Cohn 2017)
Deep Henderson (on their CD *Pyramid Strut*) (Fred Rose, 1926)
Delta Bound (Alex Hill, 1934; on their CD *Rag Band*)
Dirty TB Blues (Composed and recorded by Victoria Spivey, 1929)
Dónde Están Corazón (Luis Martinez Serrano, 1924)
Don't You Feel My Leg (Danny Barker, Blu Lu Barker and J. Mayo Williams, 1938)
Dodo Blues (C. W. Stoneking, 2006)
Do It Right (Jones, 1929)
Do Your Duty (on their CD *Six Feet Down*) (Wesley Wilson for Bessie Smith, 1933. See also *Keyhole Blues*)
Dreaming The Hours Away (Will E. Dulmage, 1927. Recorded 1928 by Clarence Williams' Jazz Kings)
Droppin' Shucks (Lil Hardin, 1926)
Dusting The Frets (Carl Davis [and the Dallas Jamboree Jug Band] 1935)
Dusty Rag (composed by May Aufderheide of Indianapolis in 1908)
Dyin' Blues (Blind Blake, 1926)
Eagle Riding Papa (on their CD *Tupelo Pine;* Big Bill Broonzy, 1930)
Egyptian Ella (composed by Walter Doyle in 1931)
Everybody Loves My Baby (1922; by Jack Palmer and Spencer Williams)
Exactly Like You (Dorothy Fields and Jimmy McHugh, 1930)
Faraway Blues (composed by Fletcher Henderson in 1920)

Farewell Blues (Schoelbel, Rappollo, Mares, 1922)
Farewell to Storyville (Spencer Williams, 1924. But he called it 'Good Time Flat Blues')
Fingering With Your Fingers (Created by The Mississippi Sheiks in 1935)
Fireworks (1928. Clarence Williams and Spencer Williams. Recorded by The Original Memphis Five and by Louis Armstrong's Hot Five)
Forget Me Not Blues (recorded - and perhaps composed - by Sara Martin in 1925)
Fourth Street Mess Around (composed by Will Shade for The Memphis Jug Band, 1930)
Freight Train Blues (on their CD *Pyramid Strut;* Recorded 1924 by Clara Smith. Composers: Thomas A Dorsey & Everett Murphy)
Frisco Bound (a 10-bar blues! Composed by Memphis Minnie and Kansas Joe in 1929)
Frog Hop (on their CD *Tupelo Pine;* Composer : Clifford Hayes, 1929. Recorded by Clifford Hayes' Louisville Stompers that year)
Frog-i-More Rag (Jelly Roll Morton, 1918)
Frosty Morning Blues (Composed by Eddie Brown; recorded 1924 by Bessie Smith; on their CD *Garbage Man*)
Garbage Man (on their CD *Garbage Man*; originally named 'Call of the Freaks' when recorded in 1929 by both the Luis Russell Orchestra and the King Oliver Orchestra)
Gee Baby Ain't I Good to You (composed by Razaf and Redman in 1929)
Give It Up or Let Me Go (Bonnie Raitt, 1972)
Gladiolus Rag (Scott Joplin, 1907)
Going to Germany (on their CD *Tupelo Pine;* Noah Lewis for Cannon's Jug Stompers, 1929)
Golden Leaf Strut (Theme from 'Milenberg Joys': Walter Melrose, Leon Roppollo, Joe Mares, Jelly Roll Morton: 1925)
Good Liquor Gonna Carry Me Down (Written and recorded by Big Bill Broonzy, 1935)

Good Time Flat Blues (Also known as *Farewell to Storyville*. By Spencer Williams, 1924)
Got a Mind to Ramble (on their CD *Owl Call Blues*; recorded by Merline Johnson in the 1930s)
Gotta Give Me Some (on their CD *Tuba Skinny*; and on their CD *Pyramid Strut*) (Composed by Clarence Williams. Recorded by Margaret Webster 1929; and also by Bessie Smith)
Grandpa's Spells (Jelly Roll Morton, 1923)
Hard Drivin' Papa (George Brooks. Recorded by Bessie Smith 1926)
Harlem's Araby (Fats Waller, Porter Grainger, Jo Trent, 1924)
He Likes It Slow (on their CD *Six Feet Down*) (W. Benton Overstreet for Butterbeans and Susie, 1926)
Hear Me Talkin' To Ya (recorded by Ma Rainey)
Hesitatin' Blues (Billy Smythe and J. Scott Middleton, 1930) (on their CD *Pyramid Strut*)
Hey Hey, Your Mama's Feeling Blue (Blind Blake's Blues - 16-bar song)
High Society (By Porter, Steele and Melrose, 1901)
High Steppin' Mamma (recorded by Cliff Carlisle in 1931)
Hilarity Rag (James Scott, 1910)
History of Man (Trinidad calypso. T.A. Codallo, 1938; recorded by Codallo's Top Hatters Orchestra)
Home (When Shadows Fall) (Harry Clarkson, Geoffrey Clarkson & Peter Van Steeden, 1931)
Honey (32-bar, a-a-b-a) (Armenter Bo Chatmon [stage name Bo Carter] recorded it in 1930s)
Honey Babe, Let the Deal Go Down (1930, Mississippi Sheiks – a 12-bar similar to 'Dallas Blues')
How Can It Be? (on their CD *Rag Band*) (Armenter Bo Chatmon [stage name Bo Carter] recorded it in 1931)
How Come You Do Me Like You Do Do Do? (Gene Austin & Roy Bergere, 1924)

How Do They Do It That Way? (on their CD *Garbage Man* and on their CD *Owl Call Blues*) (Composed by Victoria Spivey and R. Floyd, Recorded by Victoria Spivey, 1929)
Ice Man (written and recorded by Memphis Minnie 1936)
I'd Rather Drink Muddy Water (on their CD *Rag Band*; Eddie Miller, 1936)
If It Don't Fit, Don't Force It (By Barrel House Annie, 1937)
If You Don't, I Know Who Will (on their CD *Tuba Skinny*) (By Clarence Wllliams. Recorded by Bessie Smith 1923)
If You Take Me Back (recorded by Kansas Joe McCoy, c. 1934)
I Get The Blues ('I'm So Blue': Bo Carter, 1935)
I Get The Blues When It Rains (Klauber and Stoddart, 1928)
I Got a Man in the 'Bama Mines (Merline Johnson, 1937)
I Got a Woman (Ray Charles, 1954)
I Got The Cryin' Blues (on their CD *Pyramid Strut*) (probably Sara Martin and her Jug Band 1925)
I'll See You in the Spring (Memphis Jug Band, 1927)
I'm Alone Because I Love You (Irving Berlin, 1936)
I'm a Winin' Boy (Jelly Roll Morton introduced this in the 1939 documentary)
I'm Blue and Lonesome (Nobody Cares for Me) (On their CD *Blue Chime Stomp*. Georgia White and Richard M. Jones, 1938)
I'm Goin' Back Home (recorded by Memphis Minnie with Kansas Joe McCoy, c. 1930)
I'm Gonna Be a Sweet Lovin' Ol' Soul (Sara Martin and her Jug Band, 1925)
In the Gloaming (Annie F. Harrison & Meta Orred, 1877)
It's Nobody's Fault But Mine (probably Blind Willie Johnson, 1927)
Jackass Blues (Kassel and Stitzel, 1926)
Jackson Stomp (on their CD *Rag Band*) (Charlie McCoy and Walter Vincson, 1930, for the Mississippi Mud Steppers)
Jailbird (Dave Bartholomew 1955)
Jailhouse Blues (C.W. Stoneking)

Jazz Battle (Jabbo Smith, 1929)
Jelly Bean Blues (on their CD *Six Feet Down*) ('Ma' Rainey with Louis Armstrong; also Bessie Smith, 1924)
Jet Black Blues (Lonnie Johnson, 1929)
Jubilee Stomp (Duke Ellington, 1928)
Juliana (Lionel Belasco; 1937. Caribbean-style 3/4)
Junco Partner (traditional, pre-1952)
Just a Closer Walk With Thee (first recorded by a jazz band in 1941)
Kansas City Stomps (Jelly Roll Morton, 1923)
Keyhole Blues (Wesley 'Kid'. Wilson, 1927. Made famous by the Armstrong Hot Seven 1927 recording))
Kitchen Man (on their CD *Six Feet Down*) (Andy Razaf and Alex Bellenda, 1928. Recorded by Bessie Smith)
Last Night on the Back Porch (Lew Brown and Carl Schraubstader, 1922)
Late Hour Blues (Richard M. Jones; recorded by Georgia White, 1939)
Lily of the Valley (traditional; made famous by Paul Barbarin in 1951)
Lonesome Drag (on their CD *Pyramid Strut*) (Erika Lewis composed the lyrics but the tune is Vine Street Drag from 1930 - see below)
Lonesome Road (on their CD *Six Feet Down*) (Gene Austin & Nathaniel Shilkret, 1927)
Loose Like That (on their CD *Tupelo Pine*)
Love Me or Leave Me (on their CD *Tuba Skinny*) (Donaldson and Kahn, 1928)
Lovesick Blues ('I Got a Feeling Called the Blues'. Irving Mills and Cliff Friend, 1922)
Love Songs of the Nile (1933; Nacio Herb Brown & Arthur Freed)
Make Me a Pallet on Your Floor (Atlanta Blues)
Maple Leaf Rag (On their CD *Blue Chime Stomp*. Scott Joplin and Russell, 1899)
Marie (Irving Berlin, 1928)

Mary Ann (a.k.a. 'Marianne': Rafael de Leon, 1933)
Mean Blue Spirits (Spencer Williams; on their CD *Pyramid Strut;* aka Blue Spirit Blues - recorded by Bessie Smith in 1929)
Me and My Chauffeur (On their CD *Blue Chime Stomp*. Written by E. Lawler and recorded 1941 by Memphis Minnie)
Memphis Blues (W.C. Handy, 1910)
Memphis Shake (On their CD *Blue Chime Stomp*. The Dixieland Jug Blowers, 1928. Composer Clifford Hayes?)
Michigander Blues (Jabbo Smith, 1929)
Midnight Blues (On their CD *Blue Chime Stomp*. Babe Thompson and Spencer Williams, 1923. Recorded by Alice Carter in mid-1920s)
Milneberg Joys (Walter Melrose, Leon Roppollo, Joe Mares, Jelly Roll Morton; 1925)
Minor Drag (Fats Waller, 1929. On their CD *Garbage Man*)
Mississippi River Blues (Big Bill Broonzy, 1934. Tuba Skinny sometimes announce this as 'Big Boat' - the title under which the identical song was later recorded by Washboard Sam).
Moanin' The Blues
Mother's Son-in-Law (on their CD *Garbage Man*) (Alberta Nichols, music, and Mann Holiner, words, 1933)
Muddy Water (on their CD *Garbage Man*)
Need a Little Sugar in My Bowl (on their CD *Tuba Skinny*) (By Clarence Williams, D. Small, Tim Brian. Recorded by Bessie Smith, 1931)
New Dirty Dozens (Recorded by Memphis Minnie 1930; also by others, e.g. Lonnie Johnson 1930)
New Orleans Bump (Jelly Roll Morton, 1929. On their CD *Rag Band*)
New Orleans Stomp (Lil Hardin, 1923)
Nigel's Dream (on their CD *Tupelo Pine;* Shaye Cohn, 2015)
Nobody's Blues But Mine (on their CD *Garbage Man*) (Recorded by Margaret Johnson, 1925, probable composer Clarence Williams)

Nothin' [aka Dodo Blues] (C. W. Stoneking, 2006)
Oh Papa Blues (On their CD *Blue Chime Stomp*. Recorded by Ma Rainey in 1927)
Oh Red (recorded by Blind Boy Fuller as 'New Ol' Red')
Ol' Miss Rag (1915, W C Handy)
One More Thing (a simple 12-bar blues with a vocal and a break in Bars 7 - 8)
Oriental Jazz (a.k.a. 'Oriental Rag' and 'Soudan'. On their CD *Blue Chime Stomp*. Composer: Gabriel Šebek. Recorded 1917 by the ODJB)
Oriental Strut (on their CD *Owl Call Blues*) (Johnny St. Cyr, 1926)
Over in the Gloryland (Acuff and Dean, 1920)
Owl Call Blues (on their CD *Owl Call Blues*) (hauntingly beautiful Shaye Cohn and Erika Lewis composition)
Papa's Got Your Bath Water On (on their CD *Rag Band*) (Recorded by Hattie Hart and The Memphis Jug Band, 1930)
Papa Let Me Lay It On You (Credited to Blind Boy Fuller, 1938; but tune used earlier by The Harlem Hamfats.)
Pass Me Not O Gentle Saviour (William H. Doane, music, & Francis J. Crosby, words, 1870)
Peace in the Valley (on their CD *Six Feet Down*)
Pearl River Stomp (on their CD *Tupelo Pine;* Shaye Cohn, 2016)
Perdido Street Blues (Lil Hardin Armstrong, 1926)
Plow Boy Hop (Ben Tinnon. recorded by The Grinnell Giggers in 1930.)
Postage Stomp (Sam Goble and Vic Johnston, 1930)
Pyramid Strut (Shaye Cohn composition)
Redwing (Kerry Mills & Thurland Chattaway, 1907)
Right or Wrong (on their CD *Tupelo Pine.* Arthur Sizemore and Paul Biese, music, and Haven Gillespie, words, 1921)
Rock Me (on their CD *Tuba Skinny*)
Roses of Caracas (Lionel Belasco; 1928. Trinidad-style waltz)
Rosa Lee Blues (on their CD *Owl Call Blues*)

Running Down My Man (On their CD *Blue Chime Stomp*. Merline Johnson, 1936)
Russian Rag (George L. Cobb, 1918. On their CD *Rag Band*)
Salamanca Blues (on their CD *Rag Band*) (Shaye Cohn composition)
San (Michells and McPhail, 1920)
Satan, Your Kingdom Must Come Down
Savoy Blues (Kid Ory and Sid Robin, 1925)
Say Si Si (Stillman & Lecuona & Luhan, 1936)
See See Rider (Gertrude 'Ma' Rainey, 1925)
Shake It and Break It (On their CD *Blue Chime Stomp*. H. Qualli Clark & Frisco Lou Chiha, 1920)
Shine On, Harvest Moon (Jack Norworth & Nora Bayes, 1908)
Short Dress Gal (on their CD *Owl Call Blues*) (Sam Morgan, 1925)
Sidewalk Blues (Jelly Roll Morton & Walter Melrose, 1926)
Silver Bell (Percy Wenrich & Edward Madden, 1910)
Six Feet Down (on their CD *Six Feet Down*) (Erika Lewis composition)
Skid-Dat-De-Dat (on their CD *Pyramid Strut*) (Lil Hardin, 1926)
Sleepy Time Blues (Jabbo Smith, 1929. Recorded by Jabbo Smith's Rhythm Aces, 1929)
Slow Driving Moan (on their CD *Pyramid Strut*) (Closely modelled on the recording by Ma Rainey, 1927)
Slowpoke (on their CD *Tuba Skinny*)
So Long (?Bo Carter 1930)
Sold My Soul, Sold it to the Devil (Merline Johnson, 1937)
Somebody Else is Taking My Place (Russ Morgan, Dick Howard, Bob Elsworth, 1937)
Somebody's Been Loving My Baby (on their CD *Owl Call Blues*) (recorded by Mandy Lee in 1920s)
Some Cold Rainy Day (recorded by Bertha 'Chippie' Hill in 1928; probably composed by Richard M. Jones)
Some Day I'll Be Gone Away

Some Day, Sweetheart (John Spikes and Benjamin Spikes, 1919)
Some of These Days (on their CD *Garbage Man*)
Song of the Islands (Charles E. King, 1930)
Soudan (See 'Oriental Jazz' above)
South (Benny Moten, Thomas Hayes, Ray Charles, 1924)
Squeeze Me (on their CD *Rag Band*) (Fats Waller and Clarence Williams, 1925)
Stavin' Chain (Lil Johnson 12-bar song from 1937)
St. Louis Blues (W.C. Handy, 1914)
Stealing Love (Dave Nelson, 1930)
Storyville Blues (Maceo Pinkard, 1918)
Sunset Waltz (Charlie McCoy, 1929, for The Mississippi Mud Steppers. Ben Tinnon also claimed as composer.)
Sweet Lovin' Ol' Soul (Sara Martin and her Jug Band, 1925) (On their CD *Pyramid Strut*)
Sweet Mama Hurry Home (on their CD *Garbage Man*)
Sweet Potato Blues (recorded by King David's Jug Band, New York, 1930)
Tag Along Blues (Tomas Majcherski, 2017)
Tangled Blues (Shaye Cohn, 2015)
Temptation Rag (Thomas Henry Lodge, 1909)
That's It (Mississippi Sheiks, 1930)
The Girls Go Crazy (1916, attr. to Kid Ory)
Them Has Been Blues (by Will. E. Skidmore & Marshall Walker; recorded by Bessie Smith in 1925)
Thoughts (on their CD *Tupelo Pine;* Robin Rapuzzi, 2015)
Throw Your Black Hand Down
Tiger Rag (La Rocca and De Costa, 1917)
Tight Like This (Langston Curl, 1928; on their CD *Tuba Skinny*)
Till We Meet Again (Richard Whiting, words, & Raymond Egan, music, 1918)
Tin Roof Blues (Melrose, 1922)
Tishomingo Blues (Spencer Williams, 1917)
Tom Cat Blues (Jelly Roll Morton, 1924)

Too Long (recorded by The Mississippi Sheiks, 1930)
Too Much Competition (12-bar blues. Alden Bunn, 1952)
Too Tight Blues (on their CD *Owl Call Blues*)
Travellin' Blues (on their CD *Owl Call Blues*) (recorded by Jimmie Rodgers in 1931)
Treasures Untold (waltz) (on their CD *Rag Band*)
Tricks Ain't Walkin' No More (on their CD *Rag Band*) (Lucille Bogan song from 1930)
True Love (12-bar blues)
Tupelo Pine (Barnabus Jones, 2017. On their CD *Tupelo Pine*)
Turtle Blues (on their CD *Six Feet Down*)
Untrue Blues (on their CD *Owl Call Blues*) (Recorded 1936 by Blind Boy Fuller)
Up a Lazy River (Hoagy Carmichael and Sidney Arodin, 1931)
Variety Stomp (On their CD *Blue Chime Stomp*. Joe Trent, Ray Henderson, Bud Green, 1927)
Vine Street Blues (on their CD *Six Feet Down*) (possibly Benny Moten and his Kansas City Orchestra, 1924)
Vine Street Drag (Tennessee Chocolate Drops, 1930. Possible composer: J. Brown)
Viper Mad (Sidney Bechet and Rousseau Simmons, 1924)
Wabash Blues (1921 composition by Dave Ringle and Fred Meinken)
Weary Blues (Mathews, Green and Gates, 1915)
Weary-Eyed Blues (on their CD *Garbage Man*)
Wee Midnight Hours (Blind Willie McTell, 1950)
Weeping Willow Blues (on their CD *Six Feet Down*)
What If We Do? (Recorded by Katherine Henderson with Clarence Williams 1930)
What's the Matter With the Mill? (Memphis Minnie and Joe McCoy, 1930)
When My Dreamboat Comes Home (Cliff Friend and Dave Franklin, 1936)

When The Saints Go Marching In (copyright - Virgil Stamps & Luther G.Presley, 1936)
When You and I Were Young, Maggie (Their oldest tune? Composed in 1866 by J A Butterfield and G W Johnson)
Wild Man Blues (The Morton and Armstrong classic from 1927)
Willie the Weeper (on their CD *Owl Call Blues*) (Melrose, Bloom and Rymal, 1920)
Winin' Boy Blues (J.R. Morton, 1939)
Won't You Be Kind to Me? (Hattie Hart and the Memphis Jug Band, 1928)
Yaaka Hula Hickey Dula (Ray Goetz & Joe Young, music, & Pete Wendling, words, 1916)
Yearning (1925, Joe Burke and Benny Davis)
Yellow Dog Blues (W. C. Handy, 1914)
Yes Sir That's My Baby (Gus Kahn, Walter Donaldson, 1925)
You Can Have My Husband (on their CD *Six Feet Down*) (Dorothy Labostrie, 1960)
You Let Me Down (on their CD *Tuba Skinny*) (Harry Warren and Al Dubin, 1935)
Your Cheatin' Heart (Hank Williams, 1952)
You've Been a Good Ol' Waggon (on their CD *Tuba Skinny*) (Smith and Balcom. Recorded by Bessie Smith, 1925)

About The Author

Long ago, at the age of 52, Pops Coffee, who lives in Nottingham, England, began to study traditional jazz, He also eventually mastered the trumpet sufficiently well to play in a jazz band. This became the great hobby of his old age.

His other books are:
Enjoying Traditional Jazz
and
Playing Traditional Jazz.

Printed in Great Britain
by Amazon